Managing UP!

Managing UP!

59 Ways to Build a Career-Advancing Relationship With Your Boss

Michael and Deborah Singer Dobson

AMACOM

American Management Association

New York • Atlanta • Boston • Chicago • Kansas City • San Francisco • Washington, D. C.
Brussels • Mexico City • Tokyo • Toronto

This publication is designed to provide accurate and authoritative information in regard to the subject matter covered. It is sold with the understanding that the publisher is not engaged in rendering legal, accounting, or other professional service. If legal advice or other expert assistance is required, the services of a competent professional person should be sought.

Library of Congress Cataloging-in-Publication Data

Dobson, Michael Singer.
    Managing up! : 59 ways to build a career-advancing relationship with your boss / Michael S. Dobson & Deborah Singer Dobson.
        p.   cm.
    Includes bibliographical references and index.
    ISBN 0-8144-7042-4
    1. Career development.   2. Communication in industrial relations.
    3. Management.   I. Dobson, Deborah Singer.   II. Title.
    HF5381.D49   1999
    650.1—dc21   99-43413
                                                                 CIP

Printing number

10

For our parents
Barbara and Odell Dobson   Phyllis and James Singer
With love and respect for teaching us life's many lessons

Contents

Introduction   xi

1. Do Good Work   1
2. Be Supportive, Not Competitive   7
3. Get Involved in Your Profession   10
4. Observe Your Boss's Style   13
5. Give Advance Warning About Problems   18
6. Keep Your Word   20
7. Figure Out Your Boss's Likes and Dislikes   23
8. Observe Your Boss's Times of Day   28
9. Learn How Your Boss Feels About Paperwork   30
10. Make Sure You're in Tune With Your Boss's Goals   33
11. Help Your Boss Succeed   39
12. Be a "Goodmouther"   41
13. Learn How to Negotiate Like a Pro   43
14. Learn When to Fight, How to Fight, and When to Leave
    Well Enough Alone   48
15. Visit Quickly and Not Too Often   55
16. Give Negative Feedback Well   57
17. Don't Become a Threat   62
18. Accept Responsibility   65
19. Prepare for Your Meetings   67
20. Build an Appropriate Personal Relationship   72
21. Look Like a Professional   77

22. Give Credit and Praise Generously   80

23. Stand Up for What You Believe and Need   86

24. Be Informative, but Not a ''Tattletale''   90

25. Build Mentoring and Networking Relationships
    Throughout the Organization   94

26. Listen   99

27. Tolerate Some Bad Moods   101

28. Demonstrate Total Loyalty and Respect the Chain of
    Command   104

29. Learn to Handle Criticism   109

30. Get Organized   111

31. Limit the ''Great Ideas'' and Sell Them Effectively   113

32. Check Your Priorities With the Big Picture   118

33. Recognize Your Boss's Humanity   121

34. Be Aware of What's Going On, but Don't Get ''Political''   124

35. Sharpen Your Decision Skills   129

36. Consider Your Boss a Customer   131

37. Work on Better Communication   133

38. Manage Your Time Effectively   138

39. Take Your Job Seriously, but Take Yourself Lightly   140

40. Build Your Skills and Knowledge in Management   143

41. Develop Your Writing Skills   148

42. Learn How to Train Others   150

43. Arrange for Your Own Performance Appraisals on a
    Regular Basis   152

44. Write a ''5-15 Report'' Each Week   159

45. Do More   162

46. Find the Hidden Keys to the Executive Suite   165

47. Learn the Symbolic Language of the Organization   172

48. Watch the Game Film   175

49. Develop a Personal Intelligence Network in Your
    Organization   177

50. Take Care of Your Monkeys, but Don't Collect Them 182

51. Identify and Go After Important Job Assignments 186

52. Learn How to Delegate 189

53. Don't Try to Manipulate; Try to Influence, Instead 196

54. Uncover Hidden Agendas 199

55. Build Connections With Other Departments 202

56. Identify Your Boss's Allies and Enemies to Avoid
Stepping on the Wrong Toes 208

57. Ask for a Promotion 211

58. Deal Effectively With Stereotypes and Prejudices 214

59. Learn How to Deal With Problem Bosses 222

Conclusion 233

Bibliography and Suggested Reading 235

About the Authors 241

Index 243

Introduction

The parable of the gun. Imagine for a minute that you're sitting in a room with someone carrying a loaded gun, and you happen to be unarmed. That person may not harbor any ill will toward you or have any intention of shooting you. But it's hard to ignore the reality that the other person does have the power, and it's accordingly hard to be completely natural, completely at ease. The power dynamic is unequal, and that doesn't make us comfortable.

Your relationship with your boss, manager, or supervisor has the same dynamic. Your boss may be one of the world's most decent people, but regardless of actual desire or intent, your boss possesses the power to discipline you, give you better or worse job assignments, even fire you. Your boss, in other words, possesses the equivalent of that gun—and you very likely feel unarmed.

The traditional military definition of *threat* is not what most people generally mean by that word. If someone threatens us, we imagine they are demonstrating hostile intent. But the military definition is different: It's synonymous with *capability*. Someone threatens us militarily to the extent that they have the capability to do us harm, regardless of whether we believe they have a current intention to do so or not. Intentions, after all, can change. It's better to be prepared.

How can you become more secure in an environment that contains threats in the military sense—that there are people with the capability to do you harm, whether they intend to or not?

First, just because you can't have the same kind of gun as your boss doesn't mean you can't become armed yourself. Many managers have learned—some the hard way—that their employees have the power to ruin their careers and get them fired if they try hard enough. In the same way that your boss often doesn't have any intention of using the gun, you don't want to be in the business of using the gun, either. But you want to know that you're armed, not helpless.

Second, you can reduce the threat by increasing the quality of the alliance, making it clear that you are supportive, not antagonistic. You can help advance the other person's interests and goals, along with your own. When it's clear that your success and your professional growth benefit your boss, then the working relationship is good.

Third, you can deal with the interpersonal issues in a relationship, issues that sometimes make people act in ways contrary to their own best interests. In Daniel Goleman's landmark work, *Emotional Intelligence*, he writes, "[I]magine the benefits for work of being skilled in the basic emotional competences—being attuned to the feelings of those we deal with, being able to handle disagreements so they do not escalate, having the ability to get into flow states while doing our work. Leadership is not domination, but the art of persuading people to work toward a common goal. And, in terms of managing our own career, there may be nothing more essential. . . ."[1]

Your relationship with your boss. The quality and effectiveness of your relationship with your boss specifically, and the management structure of the organization generally, is the key determinant of your overall success within the organization.

The function of management is to accomplish work through the efforts of other people. Your boss's job—the job of management in general—is to develop and articulate an overall vision for that which must be done, convey that vision to the members of the team, break it down into component tasks and activities, and provide direction and enforcement to accomplish the work.

We all understand that. What we tend not to understand as deeply is that the reverse is true as well. We're managers of our own work, our own responsibilities, and our own visions. We can't accomplish our work and our objectives without the willing and voluntary cooperation of numerous people over whom we have no direct authority. Our boss is part of that number.

The concept of "Managing UP!" is that we, just as much as anyone else in the organization, have the responsibilities of management, whether our job title and job description specifies it or not.

The purpose of this volume is to equip you with at least some of the tools, resources, and understanding to help you do that part of your job in an effective manner.

1. Goleman, Daniel. *Emotional Intelligence.* New York: Bantam Books, 1995, p. 149.

What Is "Managing UP!"?

The dynamics of management. When a Roman general or emperor received a triumphal parade through the streets of Rome to show off the spoils of war, he rode proudly in his chariot while a slave whispered in his ear, "Remember, thou art mortal." It's a reminder that some of us need on a regular basis.

Nobody is really completely qualified to be a boss.

If someone becomes a manager, a supervisor, a department head, it's because that person has demonstrated some important skills and knowledge. It's almost always equally true that the new manager also lacks some qualities that are part of effective leadership. None of us are perfect.

Most managers need managing. The problem is that few staffers are in a position to provide it.

Does your manager need managing? The answer is almost certainly "yes."

Managing doesn't mean manipulating, tricking, or deceiving. Instead, it means providing the kind of support to help your boss be as effective as he or she needs to be. That helps you be more successful as well.

Mutual success through mutual management. "Managing UP!" is the act of building the kind of relationship with your manager or managers that results in mutual success. Being listened to and having your ideas respected. Getting your decisions in a timely fashion. Having the kind of influence that helps get your job and your mission accomplished.

It also means helping compensate for your boss's weak points. Everyone has them. Your boss may not be assertive enough, or may be too assertive. Your boss may not be organized enough, or may be on the compulsive side. Your boss may know the people side and have weaknesses on the technical side, or vice versa. When you can supply the missing link, you get more of what you want, need, and deserve, and so does your boss.

Self-development and growth. In addition, "Managing UP!" involves developing yourself as a professional in many ways. Expanding your skills, the range of your contacts, the level of your professionalism, all elevate you in the mind of your boss, expand your direct and indirect authority, and give you vital leverage in managing that relationship effectively.

"Problem bosses." Sometimes you may see your boss as a "problem boss"—and you may even be right. "Boss" spelled backward is

"double 'S'-O-B." The question then becomes what you plan to do about it. There's usually quite a lot you can do that is constructive, positive, and very effective in turning the situation around, or at least improving it. "Managing UP!" skills are essential for working with your boss, "problem" or not. (Though it's certainly true that when you work at building an effective relationship with your supervisor, he or she may grow much less "difficult.")

The missing link in your management plan. "Managing UP!" is often the missing link in your management plan. That's what this book is designed to help you achieve.

You may see some of the suggestions in these pages as helping the boss manage you, not you managing the boss, but remember that the two are inextricable. By building a professional reputation, by supporting your boss's interests and goals, by showing yourself to be a team player, you build the trust and mutual respect you'll need to get the support and decisions that advance your work, your projects, and ultimately your career.

You don't have to like your boss or always agree with your boss, but you need to recognize the reality of the relationship and work to make the very best of the situation.

And you *can* do it.

Why Everyone Is Ultimately in Management

Malcolm Forbes observed, "Once in a while there's wisdom in recognizing that the Boss is."

The number 1 duty of every employee is to have a successful relationship with the boss.

First, that's what you're paid for. Your supervisor sets the ground rules, the policy, and the direction for the office. Your job is to fulfill your part of the responsibilities.

Second, that's part of getting ahead. To advance in the organization, you have to show that you offer value to the organization. Value means fulfilling today's responsibilities and showing you can fulfill tomorrow's as well. Your boss determines what those are.

That's the win/win approach.

Are you in management? Perhaps you are officially a manager yourself, or perhaps you aren't a manager in the official sense. Even if you're not officially a manager, you should realize that, in a real sense, *everyone* is in management.

Let's look at management. Management is the art of getting the work done through the agency of other people. Supervisors get work done through their employees. But everyone in the organization—secretary to CEO—has to get legitimate work done through other people as well. The people through whom you need to get the work done also include your boss. You must manage your boss for your own sake, for the sake of the department, for the sake of the organization—and even for the sake of your boss!

That's why everyone—secretary to CEO—is really in management.

What work do you get done through your boss? Maybe your project involves buying a new computer, but you don't have the authority to approve a purchase order for that much money. Your boss does. When you do your homework, organize your presentation, and make your case, you're managing. That's managing up, and it's a legitimate part of every employee's responsibility.

Management isn't manipulation, management isn't trickery, management isn't abusive. (At least not necessarily.) Management is about the work, and getting the work done includes knowing how to manage up as well as down (and sideways, for that matter).

Employees always watch bosses closer than bosses watch employees. We quickly notice any deficiencies or imperfections in our boss—and there always are some, because bosses, like other human beings, are by definition less than perfect. The trouble is, your boss's deficiencies can have a big impact on you. Managing imperfect people in positions of authority becomes a critical job skill, because imperfect people are the only kind you'll ever know.

By applying the ideas in this volume, you'll be able to advance your relationship with your supervisor in a constructive and effective manner. Remember that there is nothing more important for you in terms of your long-term success and growth within any organization.

Using This Book

Managing UP! is a collection of ideas, strategies, and tactics you can use to improve your skills and relationships with your boss and others in management. The major strategies have sections of their own, with exercises and worksheets for you to use in your own self-assessment. Between the major strategies you'll find one or more "Quick Tips"—practical and immediate ideas you can use. The "Quick Tips" aren't necessarily less important than the major strategies. Sometimes, there's just less to say.

If your relationship with your boss right now isn't everything you'd like it to be, this book is a good source of ideas to help start changing it. Read the various ideas and action steps, and make the affirmative decision that you will go first in trying to change it. After all, the greatest amount of power lies within you.

Don't expect overnight miracles. If your situation isn't everything you'd like, it probably didn't get that way overnight, and it isn't likely to change overnight. Be patient with some of the changes.

Practice consistency in your efforts. While everyone has good days and bad days, and you may from time to time slip away from a good habit you've resolved to adopt, it's important to keep with it day in and day out.

Understand that it's always a two-way street, but the power dynamic between you and your boss isn't equal and never will be. In a hierarchy, rank and authority make a real difference, and if someone outranks you and is in a position of authority over you, you ultimately are the one who must learn to adapt, grow, and change. Even with that reality, there's a lot you can do.

Look around at other employee-boss relationships. You'll see that they range from excellent on down. Observe those with a strong working partnership and see what they do, paying most attention to the steps the employee takes because those are the steps that you'll need to take yourself. See how the ideas and actions recommended in this book are applied by real people in real situations. You'll learn that these ideas work and are supported in practice in every organization.

Start slow. You may find many ideas and tips that apply to your situation, but it's usually a bad tactical approach to try to make too many changes in too short a period of time. Pick one or two major areas and work on those first. As you feel comfortable with them and as you see how they work, add more. Gentle and consistent pressure over time are your best friends in accomplishing change.

When you take the right attitude, do the right work, and have some patience, you, too, will find yourself successfully "Managing UP!"

Managing
UP!

"You don't have to like or admire your boss, nor do you have to hate him. You do have to manage him, however, so that he becomes your resource for achievement, accomplishment, and personal success."

—*Peter Drucker*

Chapter

1

Do Good Work

There is no skill ultimately more important in successfully managing up than doing your job in a professional and effective manner. Good work is an example of what success expert Brian Tracy once called a "threshold skill,"[2] one that forms a foundation for everything else.

The quality of your job performance is an important lever in achieving better relationships with management. When you earn respect for your performance, you gain power and influence along with it. Your recommendations and decisions carry more weight. You become more valuable to the organization. Your comfort and personal goals become more important to management because the organization wants to keep you happy and productive on their staff. That translates into greater opportunity for promotion, salary increase, and the assignments that help you achieve them.

Conversely, deficiencies in your work product and work output can limit your ability to apply some of the other ideas in this book. People have been known to sleaze by on good personal relationships while delivering incompetent results for a while, but in the long run, the lack of performance catches up with them. Of course, good work in the absence of good relationships is also a strategy with limited application. The ideal worker delivers both.

2. Peters, Tom, and Brian Tracy. *Management Advantage*. Audiotape. Chicago: Nightingale-Conant, 1989.

Doing good work means not only delivering quality performance, but sometimes more important, knowing what quality performance is.

Consider the following steps to make sure your work is of the very best quality.

Review Your Job Description

In some organizations, job descriptions have a ceremonial role, not a practical role. You may find that your job description bears a lot or a little resemblance to what you're actually required to deliver. Nevertheless, the items in your job description form the basics of the organization's expectations. Check to make sure you're delivering the items in your job description. If there's a gap between your reality and the official description, consider asking to have your job description changed to fit the actual job.

If your job description does fit your job, make sure you are delivering in all the stated areas. Check the priorities of your different assignments and roles so you devote your attention where it makes the most difference. You may need to use better time management to focus at least some of your energies on those long-range goals.

Exceed Your Performance Standards

If your organization has official performance standards for you, check them to make sure the work you are doing fits the standards that have been set for you. What are the critical elements of the job according to the performance appraisal form? How is superior performance to be measured?

This is particularly important in cases where the official standards contain special projects or development goals to be achieved during the year. For example, if you are supposed to learn a new skill, finish a major project, or achieve a change in your performance, you need to make sure that doing it is one of your highest priorities.

Look at your performance objectives compared to the reality of your job. Again, while many organizations take the process of setting and fulfilling performance objectives quite seriously, some organizations (and some departments and some bosses) pay mostly lip service to them. Which is more true in your case?

Well-negotiated and properly designed performance objectives don't just benefit the organization, they benefit you, too. They help you prioritize and focus your work, and remove unpleasant surprises from the process of performance appraisal.

Prepare for the next cycle of performance objective setting by identifying and recommending your own objectives. Make them significant and reasonably challenging—above all, make them measurable and specific so there isn't room for disagreement about whether you succeeded or failed to meet them. If your boss doesn't particularly care about the process, the fact that you prepare the objectives in a draft form is a great labor-saving step—and accepting your objectives is easy. If your boss does care about the process, the fact that you prepare recommendations and draft copy shows that you also value the process—and accepting your input is easy.

Several times a year, take out your performance objectives and do an informal and personal performance review of yourself. How well are you doing? Where do you need to change? Seek out input from your boss about your performance against standards to make sure you are still progressing in the way your boss wants and needs. It may be that your objectives need to be adjusted midyear to keep you on track.

Don't Neglect the Swamp for the Alligators

You know the famous cartoon: "When you're up to your rear end in alligators, it's hard to remember that your original objective was to drain the swamp."

Sometimes, important elements of the job—especially those related to long-term goals—aren't being done because crises and fire fighting interfere. Try to set some time aside each day (even a little bit adds up over time) to work on any important projects. Use the "Law of the Slight Edge" to your benefit: An hour a day, each workday, applied to long-range beneficial work, adds up to 200 hours, or 25 eight-hour workdays, per year! Imagine how much you could get done with 25 eight-hour workdays to devote to long-term valuable work—and then remember that an hour a day is about the only reliable strategy to get those days.

Ask for Feedback

Doing the right thing and doing things right aren't just measured by you. Your boss legitimately has a lot of input in deciding what "right" means. The concept of "important" in an organization is always a negotiated product of what you think is important, what your boss thinks is important, what senior management thinks is important, what coworkers think is important, and what customers think is important.

Ask for feedback about your goals, your methods, and your priorities. If you do work your boss doesn't need, value, or care about—even if you do it brilliantly—it doesn't count as "good work."

Some bosses welcome your search for feedback; others may act resentful or dismissive of your attempt to get feedback. With those bosses, you may decide that it's a bad idea to solicit feedback. The more likely situation is that there is a style conflict. Some bosses may be comfortable holding a performance review meeting. Others may prefer random, brief "check-ins," in which you check in on a specific assignment. Still others expect you to read the subtle cues they put out about your performance, or to figure out what they want. Finally, some bosses have never actually figured out what they want from you, and your inquiries for feedback may be pointing out a weakness and conflict issue for them.

First see if you can adjust your style and approach so that you get the feedback you need in a way that fits your boss's approach. How do you do this? Here's a three-step process that you can use in handling a large number of situations involving your boss:

Ask

Observe

Experiment

- *Ask.* Explain your desire to have regular feedback, explain that a direct approach seems not to be working, and ask how you might be able to get the feedback you need in a style that works for your boss.
- *Observe.* Observe your boss's style to see if you can figure out strategies that might work. If any of your coworkers are able to get feedback, observe how they do it and try the same tactics.
- *Experiment.* Try different approaches until you find one that works. Accept that failures are a normal part of the experimental process.

Use the Ask-Observe-Experiment process regularly whenever a situation with your boss isn't working for you in an acceptable manner.

Set—and Achieve—Goals for Personal and Professional Development

Do a personal self-assessment and identify some developmental goals to improve the quality of your work. Even if you think you are already an outstanding performer—even if you've been told you're an outstanding performer—remember that everyone can improve.

What areas of your work are most important to improve? (Defining "most important" should obviously involve your boss's ideas, not only your own.) Could you best improve them through development of new skills, through better time management, through setting clearer or different priorities, or through making better plans?

If you're working in an organization that has practiced total quality management (TQM), you should remember that TQM isn't about some nebulous idea of perfection—instead, it's about continuous improvement. Your goal should be continuous improvement to achieve the best results.

The concept of lifelong learning—continuous education, skill development, mental renewal, and self-study—is part of virtually every program for personal or career success. There's hardly anything more important that you can do each week. In our experience as managers, we've provided training and development opportunities for staff. We have discovered that some people eagerly seek out the opportunity to learn and grow, and others only do so when coerced. Not only do the skills that are acquired help some people prosper in the organization more than others, but we've also seen that the attitudes of those who sincerely practice lifelong learning also help them stand out from the crowd.

We assume that your work is good—from your boss's perspective as well as from your own—as we explore the other ideas and steps you should follow in successfully managing up.

MY "GOOD WORK" ASSESSMENT

1. My key job responsibilities

   _____

   _____

   _____

2. Measurements of "superior" performance

    _____

    _____

    _____

3. Most critical long-term projects and goals

    _____

    _____

    _____

4. Skill areas in which I can best improve

    _____

    _____

    _____

5. My boss's top three current priorities

    _____

    _____

    _____

Chapter

2

Be Supportive,
Not Competitive

The advice to "Be supportive, not competitive" doesn't merely apply to "Managing UP!"; it's a good way to behave with co-workers and peers as well. Certainly, competitiveness is an appropriate job skill, and you want to move ahead. But the all-too-common confusion between being competitive and being cutthroat has been known to cause a rebound problem for a number of otherwise successful people.

Competition in the Workplace

In his humorous book on Machiavellian managers, L. F. Gunlicks reports the practical thinking of a good many people when he writes, "Throughout your career, with rare exceptions, you should always regard your colleagues as enemies. Especially at the beginning of your career, your colleagues are your greatest threat to promotion. Friendship is a fine thing in its place, but on the job everyone is a potential cutthroat."[3]

We don't want to go there in this book, but in all honesty there's enough truth in that observation to make it somewhat uncomfort-

3. Gunlicks, L. F. *The Machiavellian Manager's Handbook for Success*. Washington, D.C.: Libey Publishing/Regnery, 1993, p. 11.

able. In fact, there certainly can be a conflict between the goals of the organization and your own goals. But there are almost always opportunities to find common interests that enable effort toward shared goals. Making the pie larger is more important than quarreling about who gets which piece. Finding ways both parties can grow and prosper gets better long-term results than anything else. That's at the core of what's known as "win/win" negotiation, in which both parties end up getting more of what they want and what they need.

Team Playing

Your goal should always be to demonstrate that you are a team player. You do this by recognizing that the organizational reality is that you ultimately succeed by making the organization and the team successful. The ways in which that is true may not always be instantly apparent, but with thought and examination you can find them. The key question is always, "How can my interests be advanced by advancing the interests of my organization, my boss, my peers?"

The right kind of organizational competitiveness is to compete within a team structure and with team goals at the heart of what you do. In professional sports, helping the team win is often the best way to improve your own salary and position.

Think "win/win," the core concept of team participation. You win by helping others win.

This is particularly crucial in managing your relationship with your own boss. You can succeed if and only if you help your boss succeed. Look for ways to advance your own interests and goals by helping others achieve their own goals, and you'll get ahead in a way that others won't feel the need to oppose.

QUICK TIP SELF-ASSESSMENT

1. Ways in which I show myself to be a "team player"

_____

_____

_____

2. Ways in which I may appear competitive with others

    _____

    _____

    _____

3. Ideas for improving mutual support and team performance

    _____

    _____

    _____

Chapter

3

Get Involved in Your Profession

I f there is a professional or trade group in your industry you can join, join it. Go to meetings; get involved. At trade shows, set a goal of getting to know people in your industry. Not only is this valuable to your career, it's a valuable resource within your company.

Here are three of the most important benefits, both for you and your organization:

- *Networking.* You need a network of contacts both inside and outside your organization. This isn't simply a way to get a new job (though that's sometimes a benefit); it's a way to broaden your horizons and mentoring relationships.
- *Knowledge.* Whether they want to or not, organizations tend to breed a little bit of "tunnel vision" about their methods and processes. Getting to know your industry helps bring a breath of fresh air into your own company, and everyone benefits.
- *Information.* Listen carefully, read widely, and follow the trades, and you'll discover that you can learn a lot about what's really going on. Without actively spying or other ethically questionable behavior, you'll automatically learn valuable information.

While joining is the first step, participation is the next step. While it may or may not be productive or worthwhile for you to become active in the management of the group, there are normally many activities to choose from that may advance your interests and goals.

It's completely appropriate to consider your own career interests and your organizational interests in deciding how best to become involved in an association or show. Virtually everyone in the group has the same objective; in fact, the association or show exists primarily for that purpose. The trick is to find the opportunity that is simultaneously worthwhile (or at least not harmful) to the group while beneficial to your organization and yourself.

There is a level of involvement that you can simply seek out on your own, without the necessity of formal consent, though it's always appropriate to keep your supervisor informed. There is a higher level of involvement—one that may detract from your work at the organization itself or may bring your interests into conflict with those of your organization—where permission and the active support of your management is necessary.

Watch out as well for cases in which your own boss isn't involved in the industry—perhaps even thinks it's not particularly worthwhile—while people higher in the management structure are active in the association and support its goals. Try to get at least tolerance, if not active support, from your boss. You can do this by making sure that your boss shares in the benefits of your participation, say, in the form of information, and that the consequences for your productivity are minor.

Don't neglect charitable activities, especially those with some degree of corporate sponsorship. The opportunity to do well by doing good may be present. Do make sure you avoid the appearance of brown nosing. Selecting charities that put you ostentatiously in the company of the highest level of management may get you a bad reputation, even if your motives are in fact pure. Make sure at least some of your roles are the sort of roll-the-sleeves-up, get-your-hands-dirty activities that clearly aren't designed to benefit your career goals. (Though, in fact, they do.) Pay your dues, build your relationships, do good in the process.

Quick Tip Self-Assessment

1. Names of organizational and trade associations to which I can belong

    _____

    _____

    _____

2. Activities that will bring me in closer contact with others in my industry

    _____

    _____

    _____

3. Sources of information (trade journals, conferences) that will expand my competitive knowledge of my profession and industry

    _____

    _____

    _____

Chapter

4

Observe Your Boss's Style

Current psychological research tells us that people in fact have natural differences in style and temperament: the characteristics that make us as distinct individuals value and prefer different behaviors, different job assignments, different communications approaches, and different goals. People with different personality styles have different communications styles as well.

It's important for you to gain at least a basic knowledge of personality styles so you can improve your understanding of other people, work more effectively with them, solve problems and resolve conflicts with them, and thereby achieve your goals. This is particularly crucial when dealing with your own managers. To work with them effectively, you've got to know where they're coming from.

You also need to understand your own style. Like everyone else, you have preferences, approaches, and communications issues. If you find your boss difficult to relate to, the chances are he or she feels the same way about you. If you learn to relate to him or her more effectively, by the same token he or she will likely automatically relate better to you.

Noted communications expert Tony Alessandra calls this concept The Platinum Rule[4]—"Do unto others in the style they prefer to be done unto"—and this idea underlies some of the most impor-

4. Alessandra, Tony. *Mastering Your Message*. Audiotape. Mission, Kans.: SkillPath Publications, 1997.

tant ideas about communication you can find. When you deal with people who possess different styles, you should alter your own behavior to fit their style—the issues of temperament, pacing, word choice, sensory preference, emotionality—if you want to achieve maximum results.

There are many tools and systems for understanding personality types, from the Myers-Briggs Type Indicator (MBTI) to Performax DISC to the Personality Explorer model described below.

Sometimes style models and temperament theories are misunderstood as claiming to reveal "everything" about a person. Of course, no tool tells you everything you might possibly want or need to know about another human being. On the other hand, you don't need to know or understand everything; you just need to know how to adjust your style to work more effectively with specific people. When you use style models properly—as clues, not textbooks—you'll find them valuable and appropriate.

The Personality Explorer

The Personality Explorer describes four major styles, or preferences, you'll encounter in the organization, and gives you strategies to deal with them.[5]

Here's a quick summary:

- *Focusers* focus on the work, and are often direct and authoritarian in style.
- *Relaters* value human relationships and tend to have a more participatory outlook on management effectiveness.
- *Integrators* are the idea people, and they tend to want to know reasons, theory, and background. They brainstorm a lot, and challenge your ideas.
- *Operators* are most concerned with detail and procedures.

Problems in your relationships can happen because of natural style friction or style extremism. Natural style friction might happen when a goal-oriented focuser and a relationship-oriented relater try to work together, for example. Such problems can be worked out if at least one participant is aware of the source of conflict and adjusts his or her style to match. (That's your job when working with your boss.)

5. Dobson, Michael. *Exploring Personality Styles*. Mission, Kans.: SkillPath Publications, 1999, pp. 18–19.

Personality Explorer Grid

	Focuser	Relater	Integrator	Operator
Key Concern:	Focus (What)	Relate (Who)	Integrate (Why)	Operate (How)
Wants to know about the:	Task at hand	Big picture	Significance	Details
Preferred Role:	Taking charge Working independently	Coordinating Facilitating	Problem solving Diagnosis	Monitoring Analyzing
Values:	Practicality	Teamwork	Innovation	Documentation
Preferred Manage Style:	Directing (Authoritative)	Organizing (Democratic)	Planning (Self-directed)	Controlling (Systematic)
Wants to be valued for being:	Productive	Flexible	Self-reliant	Accountable
Values in other people:	Successful experience	Group participation	Questioning	Compliance
As a follower, respects:	Strong leadership	Group consensus and focus	Personal significance and good reasons	Policy, systems, laws, procedures
Works best when given:	Clear goals	Broad, general goals	Ideas and input	Systems
Management focus is on:	Outcomes	Involvement	Input	Procedures
Wants to have:	Authority	Influence	Time to assess	Clear boundaries
Learns best by:	Doing	Observing and participating	Listening and self-study	Repetition and procedures

You may also encounter style friction and style conflict working with others in your same style. For example, two focusers might fight for dominance, two operators quibble over details, two relaters compete for being most likable, or two integrators get trapped in endless arguments about whose idea is best.

Style extremism can happen when a person with a particular style is under stress and goes to the outer limits of the style. A focuser becomes a tyrannical dictator, a relater becomes everybody's buddy, an integrator transforms into an impractical visionary, and an operator turns into a compulsive nitpicker. By providing support, you can actually help someone move more toward the calmer and more productive elements of his or her normal style.

When you've gained some experience using one of the style models available, make sure you understand your own type and how it comes across to others of each different type. Practice figuring out the styles of others, making sure you don't fall into the trap of "overclassifying," or trying to pigeonhole people without regard for real individual differences. Types and styles help you understand motive and communications behavior; they don't serve as a substitute for understanding individuals as individuals.

You'll find great value in exploring this powerful topic and in improving your ability to "read" personality types in your managers and colleagues.

MY BOSS'S STYLE

Based on my observation, my boss:

- Is most concerned with (circle one)
  Results   People   Reasons   Procedures

- Cares most about (circle one)
  Immediate   Overall   Significance   Details

- Prefers the role of (circle one)
  In charge   Coordinator   Problem Solver Analyst

- Values in other people (circle one)
  Practical   Teamwork   Innovation   Detail

- Uses a primary management style of (circle one)
  Authoritative   Democratic   Self-Directed   Systematic

- Cares about others' performance in (circle one)
  Results   Teamwork   Ideas   Procedures

Add answers in each column to determine most likely personality
style (circle one)

  Focuser   Relater   Integrator   Operator

Chapter

5

Give Advance Warning About Problems

In Japanese monster movies, there's frequently a scene where the movie monster du jour (Godzilla, Mothra, Gamora, etc.) is a little baby monster. People say, "Oh, what a cute little monster!" and ignore it. They wait until the monster is full-grown and busily stomping downtown Tokyo; then they shout, "What are we going to do?"

The answer is, of course, nothing. When Godzilla is rampaging through downtown Tokyo, there's very little you can do about it. The best options are now in the past.

Know the Godzilla Principle: "The earlier you identify a problem, the more options available to solve it."[6]

The very worst thing you can do is to let your boss be blindsided or surprised by someone in senior management about something wrong. Don't ever let that happen. The way to avoid this is to spend part of your time in "baby monster patrol," or looking for things that might go wrong so you have the maximum opportunity either to fix them or at least to alert affected people.

Project management authority Alexander Laufer observes, "Do not accept project surprises as acts of God. While you cannot elimi-

---

6. Dobson, Michael. *Practical Project Management*. Mission, Kans.: SkillPath Publications, 1996, pp. 12–13.

nate all surprises, you can still anticipate many of them before they occur, leaving sufficient time to attenuate and often deaden their impact on the project. Quite often you do not have to be a prophet to perceive what the issues are before they become issues."[7]

Follow the "DBMP-BMA" rule: "Don't bring me problems, bring me answers." Recommend a solution at the same time you identify a problem; it adds to your professionalism. It's actually less essential that your answer be the best possible answer, as long as it's legitimate and you offer it up front.

This is a critical part of "Managing UP!" Mistakes and problems are an inevitable part of business, and everyone makes her or his share. The best team members are not typified so much by a lack of problems as by a proactive response to those problems. Proactivity is only an option if you've anticipated the problem in the first place.

Don't be afraid to ask for help when you need it. You'll find your embarrassment lessens tremendously when you are able to raise the warning flag well in advance of the upcoming crisis.

QUICK TIP SELF-ASSESSMENT

1. What has been my previous performance in giving early warning about problems?

    _____

    _____

2. How could I do a better job in the future in identifying potential problems in their "baby monster" stage?

    _____

    _____

3. For the next problem I find this way, how can I apply the "DBMP-BMA" approach?

    _____

    _____

7. Laufer, Alexander. *Simultaneous Management: Managing Projects in a Dynamic Environment*. New York: AMACOM, 1997, p. 240.

Chapter

6

Keep Your Word

Personal honesty is not only part of good character, it's an essential ingredient in making your professional relationships work. Your reputation for keeping your word affects how all the other strategies work for you.

Retired Speaker of the House Tip O'Neill called a colleague who'd cut $3 million from a project O'Neill favored. "It's a waste of money and we've got better things to do," the colleague replied.

"Hold on," replied O'Neill. "We were having dinner and you gave me your word you'd put that money back in."

"Well, you're a nice [so-and-so], taking advantage of me when I was half stewed," replied the congressman. "But if that's really what I said, I'll put it back in." And he did.[8]

"In politics," O'Neill observes, "your word is everything. Keep it and good things will happen to you."[9] In fact, your reputation for honesty is one of the few assets you have. Guard it at all costs.

Saying "No." Some people who have a hard time saying "no" end up saying "yes" and then not delivering. Although you may get into trouble saying "no" up front, you'll get into less trouble than you will for failing to deliver.

8. O'Neill, Tip, with Gary Hymel. *All Politics Is Local: And Other Rules of the Game.* New York: Times Books/Random House, 1994, pp. 129–130.
9. Ibid., p. 125.

Four Rules for Keeping Your Word

- *First rule: Be careful about the promises you make.* Give your word carefully and with forethought. A rash or hasty promise will come back to haunt you. As Napoleon observed, "The best way to keep one's word is not to give it."
- *Second rule: Make promises specifically, not generally.* Even if you really didn't promise what the other person perceived you promised, the other person will still consider you dishonest if you fail to deliver. Double-check to make sure you're understood properly. Confirm in writing when necessary.
- *Third rule: Make your promises closed-ended, not open-ended.* Give time limits and details. Agree on a case basis, not universally once and forever.
- *Fourth rule: "Underpromise and overdeliver."* You're never breaking your word if you deliver more and better than you said you would. Err on the side of safety with your promises.

Some people believe that making grandiose promises is a career-advancing strategy, and in the short run it can sometimes seem that way. You get immediate brownie points for a "can do" attitude and strong initiative. However, if you don't deliver, you find that the short-term benefit quickly becomes a long-term liability.

When it's beyond your control. Sometimes you can't keep a promise because something has interfered that is beyond your control. Maybe you truly thought it was possible and it was not—or at least it was beyond your abilities. If this happens, be proactive. If you can't do what you said you would do, tell people at the earliest possible moment. Tell them what you *can* do instead, and deliver. Apologize, but don't grovel—it doesn't come across as professional.

About lies and other unethical behaviors. A number of times in your career, it will seem as if lying—or any one of a number of unethical (or even illegal) tactics—would be useful. While of course we neither recommend nor condone such practices, there is something useful you can gain from having the impulse to be unethical.

When you are tempted to do something bad, there's always a motive. There's a problem you are trying to solve that doesn't seem to be amenable to ordinary methods. Instead of simply rejecting the impulse out of hand, try to take yourself into a brainstorming mode if you have the time. In brainstorming, all ideas are legitimate, even bad ones, because refusing to censor your impulses is a way to "think outside the box," to conceive of new, and hopefully better, ways to approach the problem.

In one brainstorming session on how to deal with a backlog of unsold products, a participant suggested, "Let's torch the warehouse for the insurance money!" Obviously, no one seriously considered doing so, but by playing around with the suggestion as if it were legitimate, the group eventually came up with the idea of a "fire sale."

If you don't have time to think creatively, try to resist the impulse to behave unethically anyway. If there's one thing worse than being unethical, it's being unethical *and* thoughtless. The consequences will almost certainly be worse than the ethical alternative.

Another specific danger, especially in lying, is identified by historian Al Kaltman. "The great danger is not so much that others will believe your lies, but that you will believe them, thereby preventing you from learning from your mistakes and leading you to make bigger ones in the future."[10]

QUICK TIP SELF-ASSESSMENT

1. How well do I currently follow the "Four Rules for Keeping Your Word?"

    _____

    _____

2. How am I perceived in terms of personal integrity by my boss and others right now?

    _____

    _____

3. Ideas for improving my performance in personal integrity

    _____

    _____

10. Kaltman, Al. *Cigars, Whiskey, and Winning: Leadership Lessons from General Ulysses S. Grant.* New York: Prentice Hall, 1998, p. 14.

Chapter

7

Figure Out Your Boss's Likes and Dislikes

Separate from, but connected to, the issue of personality styles is the issue of your boss's likes and dislikes. Although personality style can certainly affect those likes and dislikes, you need to observe your boss's reactions to the specific work situations that arise in your office. To build an effective relationship and gain maximum influence over your situation, you need to adjust to those likes and dislikes.

Priority Styles

A famous joke that makes the rounds in many offices is, "You can have it good, you can have it fast, or you can have it cheap. Pick two." In fact, many tasks (and all projects) involve trade-offs among what are called the Triple Constraints: Time, Budget, and Performance.

The nature of the work often determines the right trade-off to make. For example, if a building is on fire, the fire department might be able to do a better job by waiting two days for the large hook and ladder, but that's silly. If they wait until they can do the job "perfectly," it will be too late.

On the other hand, many bosses have a general style preference for one over the other. As a general rule, would your boss sooner have you be late with the report if you could significantly improve it, or does your boss appreciate an on-time or early completion even if the report might be somewhat less thorough as a result? You'll want to adjust your performance on projects and work so you deliver the right balance of time, budget, and performance.

Decision-Making Styles

Does your boss like to have consensus on major decisions, or is simple obedience enough? Consensus-oriented bosses may have long meetings and discussions to bring everyone on board; another boss may simply want your response to be, "I understand and will comply—even if I disagree." You'll need to watch the level of negotiation and participation: more for one and less for the other style.

Understanding your boss's decision-making style will greatly affect your ability to influence or even change those decisions. It's not as simple as dragging your heels when faced with a consensus-oriented boss (sooner or later, this kind of boss has a way of making sure you get with the program), or providing robot-like compliance to the more directive boss.

Instead, try these ideas. With a consensus-oriented boss, use a slower-paced style. Provide extensive emotional support while voicing your point of view on tactics and strategy. Look at the situation from his or her point of view. Show how your suggestions support his or her ultimate goals.

With a more directive boss, disagree in private whenever possible, providing active support in public. This often gets you a better hearing. Be direct, but not emotional, in stating your point of view. "That's interesting, but I guess I disagree with you." It's very important to ask for information, because this style of boss may not provide you with all the information you need to know whether or not you really do disagree. "Can you tell me more about what you're thinking/how you arrived at that decision?"

If you have "agreed to disagree," watch out for the very special risks of failing. You've been saying all along that this approach won't work. When it doesn't, rather than serving as evidence that you were right all along, instead, you find yourself implicitly accused of sabotage or neglect. To avoid this risk, back off on your disagreement early. Don't lie: Say "I'm *not* sure it *will* work," as opposed to "I *am* sure it *won't* work."

Information Styles

Does your boss like to know what's going on, or does your boss prefer to have staff be self-directed? If the former, make sure you keep your boss informed in detail. If the latter, watch to make sure you don't go for advice and assistance too often.

Bosses who like to be intimately involved in the operation want to be consulted and asked about the work—not necessarily because they question your competence to actually perform the work, but rather because they have the emotional need to be part of the process. Don't resist this; you'll only create trouble for yourself. Instead, make it work for you. On issues in which you don't have strong feelings one way or another, ask for advice and take it. "What color would make the best impression for this report cover?"

Here's a true story:

> My boss came back from a meeting spitting mad. He called me into his office and said, "I'm going to give you a good management lesson today."
>
> We had been working on a major project to open a new facility, and had made many decisions without a lot of management review. "I just presented the project to the executive steering committee. They didn't question the decisions we made—but they had a three-hour debate on what color to paint the floor!" my boss said.
>
> "Just remember this: Management has to have a role in any major decision or project, and if you don't give them one, they'll take one."

Regardless of the virtue of "good staff work," remember there are always limits, and management has prerogatives. Make sure there is an opportunity for management input, even if you have to create one. People must have their emotional needs met as well as organizational ones.

Bosses who want you to be self-directed are often themselves self-directed. The difficulty comes when they don't give you enough information to do what's right, and then they become annoyed that it wasn't right. They perceive they gave you enough information, whether they really did or not. When you get an assignment from this style of boss, look into the situation and try to organize all your questions into one session. "Here's the information I need to get this done."

Language Styles

Words don't always mean what they say. Sometimes, in fact, they mean the exact opposite. Office politics authority Andrew duBrin observes, "Managers frequently attempt to be polite by softening the language in their demands. It is important, however, not to misinterpret this softness. Keep in mind that 'If it's not too much trouble' means 'Do it and the sooner the better.' 'If I may make a small suggestion' means 'Do it this way.' 'I don't want to rush you' means 'Hurry up.' "[11]

Coping With Pet Peeves

Learn your boss's pet peeves—the little things that annoy out of all proportion to their merit. Does your boss constantly harp on your messy desk? The messy desk is a pet peeve. On the other hand, does your boss—who believes that "a clean desk is a sign of a sick mind"—tease you because your desk is always spotless? Sometimes being perceived as "too neat" translates in others' minds to you being compulsive and nitpicky, rather than well-organized and professional.

These pet peeve issues can create unnecessary and unproductive friction between you and your boss, and it's worth making minor changes in your personal style and preferences to make these issues go away.

Pet peeves can be about rational and productive issues, or they can sometimes actually support negative behavior. In the clean vs. messy desk example just described, a messy desk can actually be harmful to productivity in the office. Even if the boss's reaction to the messy desk is out of proportion to the actual productivity damage it causes, there is a core of rationality here, and you should make the necessary adjustments.

But what if your boss wants your desk to be messy when it's naturally clean? Again, look for the core of rationality. What could legitimately be unproductive about a clean desk? Arguably, a person can become so compulsive about neatness that he or she spends more time and energy in desk organization than is warranted by the payoff. Everything "just so" isn't necessarily productive to the organizational mission.

The suggestion here is to pursue the happy medium. If your style is messy and your boss is a "neat freak," you need not have a spotless desk to have a basically organized one. If your style is neat and your boss is a slob, don't turn into a slob; just let a few pieces of paper accumulate in a way that makes your office look more "lived in" without becoming chaotic. You eliminate the pet peeve without compromising productivity—or your own core values.

11. DuBrin, Andrew. *Winning Office Politics: DuBrin's Guide for the '90s.* New York: Prentice Hall, 1990, pp. 55–56.

MY BOSS'S LIKES AND DISLIKES

1. My boss's priority preferences (check one)
    Time _____   Budget _____   Performance _____
    Other priority-style issues

    _____

    _____

    _____

2. My boss's decision-making style is primarily
    Consensus _____   Directive _____
    Other decision-style issues

    _____

    _____

    _____

3. My boss's information style is primarily
    Keep me informed _____   Leave me alone _____
    Other decision-style issues

    _____

    _____

    _____

4. My boss's major pet peeves are

    _____

    _____

    _____

Chapter

8

Observe Your Boss's Times of Day

Most people have a daily energy cycle. Some are morning people; some are grumpy until at least eleven o'clock. Identify the best times to approach your boss, and use that knowledge to get a better hearing about your needs.

In addition to the daily energy cycle, there are a few other commonsense details about timing that are worth your attention:

Bad days. Some days are bad because something happened at work; other days are bad for reasons outside work. Whatever the reason, bad days have a way of spreading into other compartments of people's lives. Observe the cues that it's a bad day for your boss and avoid optional encounters that could turn negative.

Bad meetings. One important practical tip is to be careful when your boss has just come out of a meeting, especially a meeting with higher levels of management. Offer support or do a check—"How did it go?"—but don't bring up any important business until you have a sense of the postmeeting attitude.

Bad relationships. One quick way to get into a bad mood is to have to deal with someone you don't like. If you know that your boss has certain difficult relationships, don't follow an encounter with one of those people with a potentially stressful conversation with you.

Many times, the patterns are obvious with relatively light observation. If ordinary observation doesn't do the trick, keep a journal to see if you can identify patterns over time—but heed this important warning. There are lots of valid reasons to chart and record other people's behavior and actions, but if you are caught at it, you'll be in deep trouble. Unless you can be certain—absolutely certain—you can't be discovered, only do this at home. Don't ever bring the materials into the office. When they have outlived their usefulness, destroy them.

QUICK TIP SELF-ASSESSMENT

1. My boss's best and worst times of day

    _____

    _____

    _____

2. Tip-off behavior for bad times and situations for my boss

    _____

    _____

    _____

3. Approaches that work best when the boss is in a bad mood

    _____

    _____

    _____

Chapter

9

Learn How Your Boss Feels About Paperwork

I s paperwork a key part of keeping the office going, or is it a time-consuming interruption? Different bosses (and different organizations) have different attitudes about paper. By learning how your boss feels about paperwork, you can set personal priorities more effectively and also know how to be more persuasive.

Paper vs. mouth. For some bosses, sending a tightly argued ten-page memo may be the best strategy to get results; for others, it's a sure way to have your points ignored. For still others, you need to do the primary arguing in person, but you need the paper to back you up, even if the boss never actually reads it.

Memo-itis. A number of careers have been ruined because of badly written memos. Don't ever believe that memos and e-mails are informal and therefore safe to cut corners on. In fact, they may be the only evidence senior management actually sees of your work. The first rule of memos (and e-mails) is K-I-S-S: "Keep It Short and Simple." *Never* write a memo more than one page long or about more than one topic. What if you must write more than a page? Then don't call it a memo. Call it a report instead, and put a one-page cover memo/executive summary up front.

Forms and documentation. Different organizations have different natural levels of bureaucracy. Do you need forms filled out in triplicate and signed by four managers for a new stapler, or do you go out and put a new PC on your credit card and reimbursement is routine? Know not only what the organization requires, but how your boss feels about the requirements. Above all, learn how to fill out required forms properly, especially those with departmental impact such as purchase orders and personnel forms. Build contacts in the other departments to get coaching. Get your own copies of manuals and formats to learn how to do it right.

CYA paper. Sometimes you'll find a need to document that someone has given you a specific directive, or that you gave information to a certain person, because you could find yourself in trouble without that evidence. The format is called Memorandum for the Record, or Cover Your Assets (CYA).

First, make sure you know the corporate culture. Some organizations do this routinely about everything; for others, it's one step short of insubordination. In the first instance, there is no problem. In the second, use it sparingly. Remember that you can write such memos and not put them in the general file cabinet.

Some experts recommend you keep a work diary to confirm what actually happened. Always keep information factual and brief in such a diary. Use Joe Friday's "Just the facts, ma'am" approach. Don't keep the diary at the office; leave it at home. Consider destroying it after it's outlived its usefulness.

It's worthwhile to think about memos and reports as persuasive tools. One advantage of writing over talking is that you have the opportunity to think and revise until you get it just right. That provides an advantage, especially if you have difficulty being assertive in person or must deal with a fast-talking manager. But there's a disadvantage as well: More is expected of paper than speech when it comes to quality and accuracy.

Be careful. People tend to have a primary sense they feel most comfortable using. For a paper-oriented person, paper is inherently more persuasive than any other medium. But no matter how artful and beautifully structured your prose, if you're writing for someone who only likes to talk and listen, it's effort largely wasted.

The essential goal in business writing—indeed, in all communication—is to achieve some kind of change. You may want someone to *act*, you may want someone to *believe*, you may want someone to *know*. Start by figuring out what it is you want to accomplish, select the best medium of communication for the job, and then figure out the tactics and style best suited to achieve the purpose. But always start with the clear understanding of your purpose.

QUICK TIP SELF-ASSESSMENT

1. My boss's attitudes about paper

   _____

   _____

   _____

2. My personal issues about paper

   _____

   _____

   _____

3. Ideas for improving my management and handling of paper

   _____

   _____

   _____

Chapter

10

Make Sure You're in Tune
With Your Boss's Goals

ig Ziglar, noted success expert, always comes back to his key phrase, "Are you a wandering generality, or are you a meaningful specific?"[12] In fact, you'll find that everyone who teaches success or life skills comes back to another threshold skill: goal setting. Goals alone won't get you what you want—you have to work, too—but without goals, you won't know what to do or how to prioritize your efforts.

To be most effective in an organizational context, goal setting needs to be done at several levels:

- *Personal goals.* What are your goals in this position and in your career? What do you need most to achieve and learn so that you can move on to the next stage in your life?
- *Departmental/divisional goals.* What are the goals of the department or division in which you work? What does the department need to accomplish, both immediately and over the long term? Who are its customers? How does it fit into the overall organizational mission?

12. Ziglar, Zig. "How to Get What You Want" in *What the Pros Say About Success*. Audiotape. New York: American Management Association/ Simon & Schuster Audio Division, 1978.

- *Personal goals of managers.* Starting with your boss, look at the issue of personal goals of the people whose decisions affect you. How do they see their choices, opportunities, and payoffs? How do they see their relationships with one another?
- *Organizational goals/mission/vision/values.* What is the mission of your organization? How does it see itself right now in terms of its customers, its competition, and its position in the marketplace? Where would it like to be? What values and principles affect decisions and strategies in achieving that mission? How do mission, vision, and values translate into decisions?

Goals never exist in a vacuum. Think of them as a series of overlapping circles. Your own goals, both as an individual and as a participating member of various groups (department, company, etc.), interact with the goals of other individuals and their groups. You will have the best chance of achieving your personal goals if you understand the goals of other people.

Personal Goals

For the sake of your ability to manage up, you need to know what your personal goals are within the organization. Are you looking for a promotion? Knowledge? Skills? Technical challenge? Social contact? You can't very well "manage up" if you don't know what goals you want to achieve by doing so. Being purposeful about your career goals helps you in virtually every area of your work.

Ivy Haley gives this advice: "Shaping a career is a very personal matter. It involves goals focused on your strongest values and is successfully achieved through work that is meaningful and rewarding to you. . . . Decide what you can offer, and plan strategies for offering advantages and services. Develop ideas of what you can successfully deliver. Concentrate on what you can give to your work and the people you want as associates."[13]

Organizational Goals

Start your examination of goals at the organizational level. If the organization has published mission, vision, and values statements, read them and make sure you understand what they say. Be careful. Although many organizations have developed effective, meaningful

13. Haley, Ivy. *Discovering Your Purpose.* Mission, Kans.: SkillPath Publications, 1996, p. 54.

mission statements, too many have come up with public relations "hot air."

Mission statements have the same problem as lots of great management ideas: Enthusiasm is substituted for knowledge and effort. Someone attends a seminar—or, alas, reads a book—about the importance of goal setting and focus in achieving organizational success. Suffused with enthusiasm, she or he rushes back to the office to sell the new idea. Instead of being accurately presented as a useful tool, it's presented as the "magic bullet" that will somehow transform the moribund organizational culture overnight.

Instead of being a truly collaborative process, the construction of the all-too-typical corporate mission statement is collaborative only in the sense that the members of the team selected to develop it have to guess what vision or mission is in the boss's mind, with the natural result that any potential for real creative thinking is eliminated, and the goal of personal political safety becomes paramount in the mind of all participants.

The resultant product is all too often touted as a true representation of the soul of the company, presented in a public ceremony with great solemnity, silk-screened on posters and placed on every available wall surface (not to mention the backs of all business cards), whereupon everybody goes back to doing exactly what they were doing before.

W. Edwards Deming, the leading figure in the total quality management movement, listed this advice among his famous Fourteen Points: "Eliminate slogans, exhortations, and targets for the workforce."[14] Slogans, according to Deming, have never helped anyone do a good job. And because slogans are normally aimed at workers, not at management, they always carry with them an implicit message of wrongdoing or fault among the workers.

It's not that mission statements are bad or wrong, it's that they're often developed and implemented in a way that is nearly the complete reverse of what is intended. In other words, always check to see if people are really "walking the talk." Is the mission statement really used to help people in the organization make effective decisions and achieve common goals, or does the organization regularly ignore the mission statement? "We provide quality in all products and services no matter what," the mission statement reads, but the actual performance is, "Hey, the customer won't know the difference, and we'd lose money if we did the extra work."

14. Walton, Mary. *The Deming Management Method*. New York: Perigee, 1986, pp. 76–77.

The real organizational mission is the values and goals actually practiced by senior management, not what someone posts on the wall or distributes on the back of business cards. You need to have a real sense of what the organization truly believes and practices. Make sure you take that into account in your own goal setting.

By the way, if you find major cognitive dissonance between the official mission statement and the real behavior, you won't make very many friends by pointing it out. Accept the reality that some people tend to see themselves as a little better than they really are, and push gently and consistently for better performance. Remember that in any organization, management controls the system—because that's what management is—and you can't change what you don't like about the organization without the cooperation and consent of management. You can do it, but normally not overnight. Patience, self-discipline, and the skills of managing up are the only approach that will work.

Departmental Goals

What is the goal and mission of your department? Is it a line or staff department?[15] How is the success of your department measured? Is the primary measurement internal (your boss decides) or external (other departments decide)? How is your department perceived right now by the organization as a whole? How would it like to be perceived? What specific improvements would have the strongest impact? Most important, what is your job and how does it fit into these departmental and organizational goals?

In determining your departmental goals, what your boss thinks and believes is crucial. Determine how you would answer those questions; then determine how your boss would answer those questions. If you have no idea how your boss feels or what your boss believes or thinks about these issues, it's critical that you find out. Use the Ask-Observe-Experiment approach. Ask, either privately or at a meeting. Emphasize that you want to make sure that your performance supports the real goals of your department. As with organizational goals, pay attention to any differences between what is

15. A line department participates in the strategy, design, manufacture, marketing, and service of the products and services of the organization. A staff department provides support for the line departments. Line departments include engineering, sales, marketing, manufacturing, and customer service. Staff departments include human resources, accounting, purchasing, and information technology.

said and what is done. Try new approaches and small pushes to see what you can achieve.

Your Boss's Goals

Your boss has departmental goals and personal goals. In fact, certain departmental goals may be chosen because of their impact on his or her personal goals.

Is your boss a "comer" in the organization, someone who will likely be tapped for future advancement and leadership roles, or is your boss likely settled in for the rest of his or her career? If the latter, is it voluntary or involuntary? Is your boss motivated by advancement (let's make changes and grow) or security (let's play it safe and avoid rocking the boat)? Does your boss have good relations with his or her boss and others in senior management, or does tension exist? Are there personal or interdepartmental feuds going on that you need to be aware of?

Your challenge is to figure out how you can achieve your goals by helping your boss achieve his or her goals. Marilyn Moats Kennedy, managing partner of CareerStrategies and noted authority on office politics, defined it, "What exactly can I do for you that will make you want to do it my way?"[16] In other words, a strategy of negotiation and mutual support is a fundamental asset in the political environment that exists in every organization.

When you analyze your own goals, both for advancement and for performance within the job, you need to check against the other goals that necessarily affect you. In learning to manage your boss and others, you must understand how they see the situation and their own interests so you can work to achieve win/win outcomes, the only way to achieve your long-term goals.

GOALS SURVEY

1. The mission of my organization

    _____

    _____

    _____

16. Kennedy, Marilyn Moats. *Office Politics*. Audiotape. Chicago: Nightingale-Conant, 1989.

2. The mission of my department

    _____

    _____

    _____

3. The mission of my job

    _____

    _____

    _____

4. My boss's top organizational priorities

    _____

    _____

    _____

5. My boss's top personal priorities

    _____

    _____

    _____

Chapter

11

Help Your Boss Succeed

One of the single most powerful success strategies anyone can follow in the art of managing up is to help your boss succeed. This involves not only solving—better yet, avoiding—problems, but also supporting the overall strategic direction and vision of your boss.

Anyone—including your boss—can get into trouble from time to time. One way to do your job the right way and help your personal and professional goals at the same time is to be right there to help. Don't always wait to be asked or ordered; volunteer to help out, and then make sure all the credit goes to your boss. In the long run, that's a strategy that will benefit you both. Management expert Andrew DuBrin observes, "When you are caught up in the pressures of pursuing your own ambitions, it is easy to forget the primary reason you were hired: Your prospective boss thought you could help accomplish the department's objectives [and] contribute directly or indirectly to his or her success."[17]

To achieve this, make sure you have a good command of your boss's goals as well as departmental and organizational priorities. Using the Godzilla Principle, (Chapter 5) work at anticipating problems before they occur to give you the maximum opportunity to be proactive.

17. DuBrin, Andrew. Op. cit., p. 58.

Keep track of major projects and initiatives in your department whether or not they fall primarily in your sphere of work or influence. You can do this informally; you don't necessarily need to have full expert knowledge of everything (and trying to get it may provoke a suspicious reaction). Listen in staff meetings to everything that's going on.

Don't look like you're trying to amass personal credit or brownie points. Your sincerity and desire to help in a selfless, altruistic fashion counts for a lot. If your help is rejected, back off. Don't force it on anyone, coworker or boss. Don't look for any credit afterward—but don't worry. You'll benefit in the long run.

QUICK TIP SELF-ASSESSMENT

1. Areas in which my boss particularly needs support

    _____

    _____

    _____

2. Ego issues and problems my boss may have in accepting support

    _____

    _____

    _____

3. Ways I can provide support in a more effective manner

    _____

    _____

    _____

Chapter

12

Be a "Goodmouther"

Yes, you should talk about people behind their backs—the trick is to say only nice things. You know from experience that things that are said behind others' backs have a way of getting back to them. In fact, the normal reaction is to take that information far more seriously than whatever has been said face-to-face. As George Herbert said, "Good words are worth much, and cost little."[18]

You can use that reaction to your benefit by saying positive things—being a "goodmouther," rather than the more common "badmouther."

When someone compliments you on a project or other activity done as a team, accept the compliment by saying "Thank you." Don't turn the compliment away or make it sound as if you had nothing to do with it. Then say, "Mary gave me some great ideas that helped me do it." Of course, only say this if in fact Mary gave you great ideas. Give only honest praise.

When a name comes up in conversation, say something complimentary. "You know, Jack is always first in with his sleeves rolled up whenever there's a problem." Again, say this only if it's an honest description of Jack.

18. Herbert, George. Quoted in Fielder, Barbara, *Motivation in the Workplace*. Mission, Kans.: SkillPath Publications, 1996, p. 18.

QUICK TIP SELF-ASSESSMENT

1. How good a "goodmouther" am I?

    _____

    _____

    _____

2. Ways in which I can do a better job talking about people
    behind their backs

    _____

    _____

    _____

3. Specific things I can say about others

    _____

    _____

    _____

Chapter

13

Learn How to Negotiate Like a Pro

Negotiation is such a fundamental skill that it's nearly impossible for you to succeed long term without developing skills in this area. Unfortunately, many people get the wrong idea about what negotiation is and how it works. The concept of win/win negotiation, which has been extensively written about, is often—mistakenly—thought of as soft at best, ineffective and self-destructive at worst. The problem is, this misunderstanding leads people into a very difficult internal contradiction.

The distaste that some people feel for the concept of negotiation results from seeing negotiation as win/lose (I win/you lose) or lose/win (I give up rather than make an enemy out of you) rather than win/win (we both come out of the negotiation with our needs met). That's a terrible choice. We can behave cruelly or unethically and get what we want, or be nice and reasonable and get the shaft in the process. No wonder that many people run screaming from the room at the thought of negotiation, or that others decide, "If it's a dog-eat-dog world, I'm going to be the dog that eats!"

The problem is that we too often think of negotiation simply in terms of the used-car-salesman model, in which neither party will see or have to deal with the other one after the end of the negotiation. But most of the people with whom we negotiate are people we have to work with and live with after the fact. In addition to our moral or ethical qualms about using "hard" negotiating strategies, the reality is that if we leave someone unhappy, that person is unlikely to forget. As the saying goes, "Never leave a wounded enemy on the field of battle with the incentive to return and seek revenge." We will have to deal with the leftover negativity at some future time.

Win/win approaches aren't just nice, they're necessary for our long-term relationships and performance.

But how is it possible to negotiate and have both parties win?

Understanding Win/Win

Negotiation isn't simply about compromise (let's just split it 50-50). While sometimes a compromise solution in which each party gives a little bit is acceptable, often a compromise turns into lose/lose.

Roger Fisher and William Ury of the Harvard Negotiation Project point out that in many negotiations the participants see a fixed "pie," but that it's often possible to expand the "pie." They tell the story of "the proverbial sisters who quarreled over an orange. After they finally agreed to divide the orange in half, the first sister took her half, ate the fruit, and threw away the peel, while the other threw away the fruit and used the peel from her half in baking a cake."[19]

In other words, common sense would suggest that the orange could only be split in such a way that the parts added up to 100 percent, but this particular orange could have been split 100-100, not 50-50, because the two sisters had different yet complementary interests!

The win/win concept of negotiation emphasizes that preserving the relationship is an important goal in most negotiations, and that's particularly crucial when the other participant in negotiation happens to be your boss. You might be able to force your desires through his or her resistance, but you have to expect him or her to remember that in the future. "If you wrong us," Shylock says, "shall we not revenge?"[20] Win/win isn't only ethically superior, it's more practical as well.

"Hard" vs. "Soft" Styles

You can make a lifetime study of negotiation, and it will benefit you in every area of your life. It's worth adding to your list of areas for

19. Fisher, Roger, and William Ury. *Getting to Yes: Negotiating Agreement Without Giving In.* New York: Penguin Books, 1981, p. 59.
20. Shakespeare, William. *The Merchant of Venice.* Act III, Scene 1, Line 65.

personal and professional development, because you will ultimately find yourself in continual negotiation situations. Negotiation styles are sometimes divided into "soft" and "hard," but that's not a very meaningful distinction. Soft negotiating techniques involve collegiality and teamwork, a mutual commitment to problem solving. Hard negotiating techniques focus more on being tough and sometimes on being manipulative to get results. But the choice of tactics—soft or hard—is usually a secondary issue. The primary issue ought to be the extent of the negotiators' commitment to achieve an outcome that works for both participants. That's ultimately as much in your best interest, if not more so, than winning on every little point and squeezing the last drop of blood from your opponent.

Some Key Principles of Win/Win Negotiation

As you study negotiation skills, you'll find that different authorities have certain specific detailed and tactical suggestions. However, some general principles of effective negotiation are common to the various styles and strategies.

   1. *Do your homework.* Before negotiating anything with anybody, there are a couple of things you should do.

   First, analyze your own goal, making sure that you focus on your *interests* (the reasons you want what you want) instead of only your *positions* (the specifics for which you're asking). The position of the sisters was that each wanted the orange. To find the underlying interests, you focus on *why*. Why do you want the orange? What exactly would you do with it if you had it all? What would not be useful or necessary for you?

   Second, determine your bottom line. What do you need—and what is the best you can do assuming that the negotiation goes nowhere? You need to know this so you'll know when you're getting results, and so you won't take an offer that's less than what you'd get if there is no deal. Fisher and Ury call this your "best alternative to a negotiated agreement" (BATNA). You'll also find it referred to as "walk-away power," which belongs to whichever party has the best option to stand up and walk away from the negotiating table.

   Third, put yourself in the shoes of the other person and do the same thing. The more you understand the interests and goals of the other participant—and his or her own BATNA or walk-away options, the easier you'll find it to locate win/win options.

2. *Listen—for the real issues.* Being a good listener is a valuable negotiation technique for several reasons. First, your understanding of the other person grows, which helps you in working toward the best outcome. Second, when you listen, you automatically validate the other person, lowering his or her stress and emotionality, and create a climate in which better results can occur. Paraphrase what you're being told to make sure you understand it fully.

3. *Be persistent and patient.* You want to negotiate in order to achieve results for both parties. Surrendering and giving in are examples of lose/win, not win/win strategies. Keep your dignity and your personal strength intact by refusing to yield to hardball tactics and pressure. One reason to study such tactics yourself is that it becomes easier to counter them in practice.

Being in a hurry to reach a deal often gives you a worse deal than you'd get with patience. If a particular round of negotiation isn't panning out successfully, maybe it's time to walk away for now, think about what you've learned, and try again later.

4. *Be clear and assertive.* You've heard it said, "If you don't ask, you don't get." That's true even in cases in which the other person isn't necessarily hostile or negative to your interests. If you don't ask, there is a good chance the other person doesn't even know what it is you want—and if he or she doesn't know, how can you expect him or her to read your mind? One of the most interesting elements of preparing well for a negotiation is how often you get your needs met without actually encountering the resistance you expected!

5. *Allow face-saving.* When a negotiation or conflict situation ends up putting one person "in the wrong," don't be surprised if that person feels negative about it. Feeling embarrassed or humiliated is not a positive emotion. When you must show your boss that he or she is incorrect, or has made a mistake, or has made a bad decision, you not only have to get the situation corrected, you have to resolve the emotional issues in a way that allows your boss to save face.

Some techniques for face-saving include the third-party appeal, in which you don't say, "I'm right, you're wrong," but instead find a neutral third party (such as a reference book) that you'll use to resolve the issue. Another valuable technique is privacy. It's easier to admit to one person that one is wrong than to admit it publicly to everyone. A third is to find a way to allow the person to be partially right, or to allow yourself to be partially wrong. (At the least, you can always allow for the possibility of improvement.) No matter what, never gloat afterward.

You negotiate every day of your life and with all the people in your life. Don't wait until you are in a major conflict situation with the power dynamic stacked against you to develop this skill.

NEGOTIATION PREPARATION WORKSHEET

My goal (position)

_____

_____

_____

Why I want it (interests)

_____

_____

_____

What I see the other person wants (position)

_____

_____

_____

Why they want it (interests)

_____

_____

_____

Options to expand the pie (achieve win/win)

_____

_____

_____

Chapter

14

Learn When to Fight, How to Fight, and When to Leave Well Enough Alone

As the Alcoholic's Anonymous prayer says, "God grant me the serenity to accept the things I cannot change, the courage to change the things I can, and the wisdom to know the difference." Some fights matter; others don't. Assess: What is at stake? What are the odds I can win? What are the consequences if I lose or don't fight? What are the positive consequences if I win? What are the negative consequences if I win? How well could I do if I didn't fight at all?

Should you fight at all, especially with your boss and others in senior management? The answer, surprisingly, is "yes"—though, of course, it's a qualified "yes." First, remember that fights and fighting don't always have to be negative, hostile, or oriented toward the infliction of damage. Instead, think of them as tough negotiations in which people of strong opinions must somehow settle their differences and choose a course of action.

Second, a willingness to fight about an issue is often the cue someone needs to discover that you're serious and committed to an issue or point of view. It would be nice if human nature weren't this way, but with many people and many situations, whether you're willing to fight is used to determine your credibility or sincerity. The good news is that once you've demonstrated that you are willing to fight when necessary, a tactically raised eyebrow can say everything that you need said.

Third, business has traditionally been an arena in which certain macho behavioral patterns are used to determine status, position, and even professionalism. In other words, some people determine who you are by pushing you. If you back up or fall down, you must be a wimp. On the other hand, if you come out swinging, you're a threat. The assertive reaction, to stand up, to push back when necessary, and, above all, to depersonalize such situations, shows you to be made of management material. It's a game, and sometimes it may be a silly game, but don't forget there's substantial reality in it as well.

Let's look at some general principles of fighting.

- *Make sure your fights are about principle, not personal gain.* (If personal gain is a side benefit, that's fine.) Focus on organizational benefits, team benefits, customer benefits.
- *Make sure your fights are impersonal.* Remember the slogan, "Handle people with kid gloves, but issues bare fisted." Listen well to other points of view to make sure you understand them thoroughly.
- *Learn to use anger appropriately.* Anger is a legitimate business tool if used properly. First, distinguish between getting angry and losing control of your temper. Getting angry is far more legitimate. You know people who lose their temper completely and bellow their rage at the handiest target. While it's a fact that the enraged person is normally placated and often seems to win the current encounter, that person leaves resentment and negativity in his or her wake. That can come back to haunt you later. Controlled anger, on the other hand, doesn't become disproportionate to the issue at hand, stops short of eviscerating the other person, and is targeted to achieve your goal with minimum collateral damage.
- *Never forget the face-saving needs of opponents.* Work to provide them with an ego-salving way to accept your position. Making minor modifications in your idea that don't affect the substance is often a useful way to go. Listen for their issues to see if it's possible to meet their needs while still having it go your way.
- *Learn how to lose gracefully.* While tilting at windmills is occasionally necessary to preserve your integrity, you are doomed to failure when you try. When you know that further pushing will not

achieve good results, learn to let it go. You don't have to change your mind, but you do have to accept that a decision has been made and that it is not the decision you want.

- *Mend fences after any fight.* Opponents are not necessarily enemies. An opponent disagrees with you on the issue, of course, but enemies are ones with whom you also have a negative relationship. That makes it personal. You can often work with opponents and strategize toward mutually successful outcomes, but enemies are far more difficult and consequently far more dangerous. Try to keep opponents from becoming enemies, and work to turn enemies into merely opponents. Find points of agreement, and find ways you can legitimately support those who were your opponents. The subject of the fight will eventually recede, but you still need the relationships.

Choosing Your Fights

Is this your fight, or can you avoid it? Let's look at some issues for determining the right approach.

What is at stake? The stakes in the fight have to be significant before there's any sense in getting involved. There is a price to pay for fighting. A fight isn't just a fight; it's a precedent. Regardless of the individual merit of each fight, if you're perceived as being in too many of them, your overall reputation will suffer.

How does it affect or involve you personally? "I don't have a dog in that fight," goes the old Southern aphorism. While it may seem noble and appropriate to pick up the cudgel on behalf of someone else's fight, you should be careful and thoughtful before doing so. People can usually take care of themselves, and sometimes an unwillingness to fight is a strategic decision, not only a sign of weakness. It will damage your organizational reputation to be perceived as someone who charges into other people's fights like a bull in a china shop.

How does it affect your boss or other key players? It's not only your reputation at stake in a fight, it's your boss's as well. Your boss legitimately gets credit for your successes; he or she also gets the blame for any trouble you cause. It's not enough for your boss to agree with your position; you need to select fighting strategies and the lengths to which it's appropriate for you to go in order to win based on consideration of how you'll be seen as a representative of your department and your boss.

Do you have any obligations to others here? There are times you do have to stand up and be counted in someone else's fight. Be careful about accepting help from others, because you may be asked to help them at a time that's awkward or inappropriate for you. On the other hand, loyalty is an obligation, and when you've committed yourself to support someone, or when you have a debt of honor that must be paid, you must stand up on his or her behalf. There is an option, however, when you must get involved in a fight that isn't ultimately your own: You may be in a good position to serve as a broker, someone who can get both sides negotiating.

Strategies for Fighting and Conflict Resolution

There are two variables you need to consider whenever you're in a conflict situation: your concern for the other person's needs and goals, and your concern for your own needs and goals. How you balance these concerns determines the overall strategy you'll pursue. All of these strategies have their time and their place, though in general the strategies of collaboration and negotiation produce the best long-term results. Let's look at each strategic option in terms of the situations to which it is best suited.

- *Low Concern for Others/Low Concern for Self.* The strategy of simply avoiding the conflict is legitimate when the problem is relatively trivial and the potential cost of resolving it is high. "Don't make a federal case of it" is a saying that is often applied to this sort of situation. Making an issue of principle out of a little conflict is a self-defeating strategy. On the other hand, even a mutual agreement to ignore a significant issue simply makes it stick around until it finally becomes unbearable. A lose/lose strategy, which it then becomes, is when both participants value avoiding conflict over solving problems.
- *High Concern for Others/Low Concern for Self.* Giving in to the other party can be productive when the cost to you is minimal and the importance to the other person is high, and when building and supporting the immediate relationship outweighs the benefits of solving the problem. This is particularly valuable as a problem-solving tool when the other person cares a lot more than you do. If you give in cheerfully, it's tactically worthwhile to call attention to your self-sacrifice on the matter so that later, when the positions

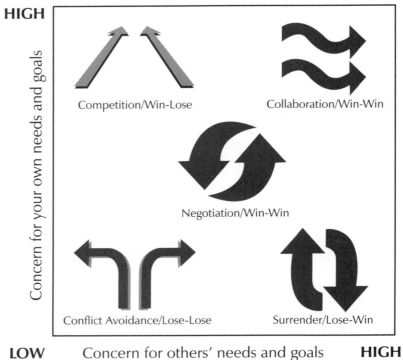

HIGH

Concern for your own needs and goals

Competition/Win-Lose   Collaboration/Win-Win

Negotiation/Win-Win

Conflict Avoidance/Lose-Lose   Surrender/Lose-Win

LOW   Concern for others' needs and goals   **HIGH**

Figure: Conflict Resolution Model

are reversed, you have. On the other hand, if you fail to satisfy your own needs and those needs matter, that's a lose/win strategy. Again, avoiding conflict at the price of your own success and goal achievement normally doesn't even achieve the goal of avoiding conflict, because you teach the other person the lesson that you can be pushed around.

- *Low Concern for Others/High Concern for Self.* This strategic scenario obviously describes what's wrong with a lot of fighting behavior in organizations. Fighting to achieve your goals while defeating the other person is appropriate in emergencies, because there is no time, and it is often the appropriate and necessary way for you to enforce rules. If someone wants to come to work late every day, while you want the person to come in on time, one person will win and the other will lose. A compromise or happy medium isn't possible in every situation. It's appropriate in that case for the organization and its management to win. On the other hand, leaving people feeling defeated can promote a later desire for retribution and even revenge. Remember, making the other person into a loser when the relationship is important and ongoing is not in your best interest.

- *Medium Concern for Others/Medium Concern for Self.* Compromise or a negotiated outcome, in which each participant gives somewhat so that both people are at least partially satisfied, can be a valuable outcome. For example, in the tardiness example cited previously, if flexitime is an organizational option and can help resolve the problem, the problem goes away. Management has given a little, and the team member has given a little, and the problem goes away. It may well be desirable for each person to be mildly disappointed if the relationship can be preserved and the outcome can be acceptable. Each side gives somewhat to achieve an acceptable, if not ideal, outcome, in what is called a win/lose-win/lose approach. One big problem with a compromise orientation, though, is that it tends to focus attention on the direct axis of conflict, and is seldom creative. Remember that brainstorming additional options and a wider way of looking at the situation often makes better outcomes possible.
- *High Concern for Others/High Concern for Self.* The goal of a win/win approach involves the application of negotiation skills, understanding, listening, and creative brainstorming to come up with the best answers. The disadvantages of the method are, first, that it is time-consuming, and, second, that it is not possible in every situation to achieve an ideal outcome. Still, it builds consensus for the long term, and when it works, the solutions are often outstanding, long-lasting, and better for both parties.

QUICK TIP SELF-ASSESSMENT

1. My track record in fighting within the organization

_____

_____

_____

2. Ways in which I have succeeded in fights

    _____

    _____

    _____

3. Ways in which I need to improve in fights

    _____

    _____

    _____

4. Ways in which I can use a wider set of conflict resolution
    tools to achieve better outcomes

    _____

    _____

    _____

Chapter

Visit Quickly and Not Too Often

Watch out for the tendency to keep going into your boss's office. It seems like a good strategy to get "face time" with the boss, but you can easily become known as a time-waster. If you have something you need from your boss but it can wait, save up five or six different items, schedule time, and do it quickly. Show respect for your boss's time. It makes a difference.

Set an agenda for each trip into your boss's office, just as if it were a formal meeting. Consider your overall purpose: Do you need decisions made, forms signed, approvals on minor issues, approvals on major issues, discussion and feedback on job-related matters, emotional reassurance, or relationship building?

How does your agenda affect the timing: Do you need to make an appointment or should this be a walk-in? Is it important that your issue be resolved right this very minute, or can you adjust your timing to take advantage of your boss's preferred times of day?

Make notes in advance about your agenda items to improve speed and efficiency. Have pen and paper handy to write down next steps, instructions, and information. Adjust the amount of small talk to fit the situation, your boss's personal style, and mood—sometimes more, sometimes less. Wrap it up by saying "thank you."

Quick Tip Self-Assessment

1. How often do I visit my boss's office, and how long do I stay? (Measure this over a period of two weeks.)

   _____

   _____

   _____

2. Are there ways to shorten and lessen those visits in a positive way, while still getting the work done?

   _____

   _____

   _____

3. Ideas for implementing the techniques in this section

   _____

   _____

   _____

Chapter

16

Give Negative Feedback Well

From your own experience, you know that inept criticism—poor ability to provide negative feedback—is one of the most damaging and destructive forces at work in the organization. It's tough enough to receive criticism, and even tougher to do something that we all must do sooner or later—give effective negative feedback to the boss. That's an essential element of managing up.

By effective, we mean several things. First, of course, is that the boss or manager (or anyone else, for that matter) makes at least some improvement or positive change as a consequence of the feedback. Second, when providing negative feedback to someone higher on the management ladder, we'd like to keep our job.

This is possible because although all criticism is negative feedback, not all negative feedback falls under the heading of criticism. Your skill in this critical area is essential to your success in managing up. Negative feedback is a necessary part of assertive communication. If you can't tell your boss what he or she needs to change, it's unlikely the change will come about.

Two ingredients work well together to lower the risk and increase the likelihood of a positive outcome from negative feedback or criticism: behavioral language and the Negative Feedback Model. Both strategies involve advance preparation on your part to ensure success.

Behavioral Language

Knowing how to set up your negative feedback in behavioral, rather than judgmental language, is the first and fundamental skill.

The judgmental approach assumes we already know the underlying cause of the behavior. "My boss is out to get me." "My boss said that just to humiliate me in public." Not only might you be wrong, but when you give feedback in judgmental language, you provoke argument and denial, rather than achieve results.

What behavior made you conclude that your boss is out to get you? Did your boss change a decision you made? Has your boss said critical things about you in a public setting? These things might mean that your boss is out to get you, but they could have other explanations as well.

More important, which approach do you think will work better in dialogue: "You're out to get me and I want to know why" or "Yesterday, when I told you what I had done to resolve the problem on the Smith account, you called the client directly and changed the decision. The impact of this is that the client doesn't want to accept my decisions, which is making more work for you as well as me. It also made me feel undercut and not trusted. I'd like to know what your intention was so that we can avoid this situation in the future." Obviously, the second approach is far more likely to open a real dialogue.

One of the key principles of communications effectiveness is that if you can't describe a problem in behavioral terms, you're unlikely to get any change.

Negative Feedback Model

Plans and models help you get prepared for difficult and stressful communications situations, and giving negative feedback to a superior is certainly difficult and stressful. The five-step Negative Feedback Model[21] is a tool to help you plan your approach and get a workable solution that both you and the other person can live with. Make sure each step is complete before moving on to the next. Be clear in your mind what you want the outcome to be.

1. *Define the problem in behavioral terms.* Start by writing down your concern or problem, using the exercise at the end of this chap-

21. Dobson, Michael Singer, and Deborah Singer Dobson. *Coping With Supervisory Nightmares.* Mission, Kans.: SkillPath Publications, 1997, pp. 21–23.

ter. It's fine if the first draft is highly judgmental. Identify your judgmental issues (My boss is scheming to undercut me), convert them to behavioral language (On Tuesday, my boss changed my decision about the Smith account by calling the client directly without telling me), and use that behavioral description to open the negative feedback dialogue. Be specific and list as many details as you can. Be calm, and talk honestly and openly about your observations.

Won't this get you into trouble? In all honesty, there are some bosses and managers you can't approach at all without provoking some sort of reaction. But by rephrasing your issues and concerns in behavioral (descriptive) language, you remove a lot of the implicit threat and accusation from the message. That lets most people hear what you're saying without as strong a reaction, which dramatically increases the likely success of your communication.

2. *Relate the impact and your feelings.* Describe the impact of the behavior, both on yourself and on others. Impact can be external (interfered with work) or internal (emotional). You need to describe both elements. When you describe your feelings, make sure you state them as "I" messages: for example, "When you check each step of the work as I do it, *I feel* that I'm not trusted," as opposed to "When you micromanage everything I do, *you show* you don't trust me."

3. *Ask—then listen for the real problem.* Allow the other person to talk about the situation from his or her point of view. Sometimes, people need to make excuses or vent their feelings before they can accept the necessity for change. Let them. You can listen to people and accept their feelings without necessarily agreeing with them. This is also the only way you can find out the reasons or motives for their behavior. Avoid questions that begin "Why?" and closed-ended questions (those answered "Yes" or "No"). These only cause defensiveness. Instead, ask questions like, "What were you hoping to achieve?" or "What did you intend when you did that?"

4. *Work out a win/win change.* Negotiate next steps to be taken. What are actions on which you can both agree? Look for choices that will correct the problem, both now and in the future, focusing on the win/win approach outlined in Chapter 14. Make sure planned steps are cast in behavioral, observable, and measurable terms.

5. *Focus on the positive elements of the relationship.* Negative feedback, no matter how well expressed or how carefully phrased, is difficult to take, and it's made more difficult by differences in rank.

Your boss may feel that the idea of accepting criticism or admitting error shows unprofessional weakness, or that it will result in loss of respect and authority. Make sure you emphasize the positive elements of the relationship. End with a positive comment. Of course, you can't lie, sugarcoat, or be hypocritical in your positive comment. One more reason to plan your approach before having the dialogue is to give you a chance to identify honest positives.

GIVING NEGATIVE FEEDBACK

JUDGMENTAL vs. BEHAVIORAL LANGUAGE
Write down your situation as you perceive it. It's okay to use judgmental language to start.

_____

_____

_____

Now look for judgmental language (presupposes motive) and change it to behavioral description (describes observable behavior).

Judgmental Language   Behavior You Actually Observe

1. _____   _____

2. _____   _____

3. _____   _____

NEGATIVE FEEDBACK MODEL

1. Define the problem in behavioral terms. (Use the information from the previous step.)

_____

_____

_____

2. Relate the impact and your feelings.

    _____

    _____

    _____

3. Ask—then listen for the real problem.

    _____

    _____

    _____

4. Work out a win/win change.

    _____

    _____

    _____

5. Focus on the positive elements of the relationship.

    _____

    _____

    _____

Chapter

17

Don't Become a Threat

You can be perceived as a threat—or even *be* a threat—to your boss without ever intending to, or sometimes without being aware of it.

Conflicts and Threats

Sometimes, you may work for a boss who provokes conflict and get into a fight. If you lose, it's bad enough. But sometimes winning can be even worse. As we've discussed in writing about negotiation and conflict, you often have to maintain a relationship with someone after the conflict or negotiation is resolved. Winning isn't really winning if you've made an enemy or revenge-seeker out of someone with the power to promote or punish you.

The goal of not being a threat doesn't have to be identical to not having any conflict at all. Even if you are willing to be simply submissive, that often isn't enough. A person who will bully you until you fight back and then try to destroy you will also despise and be contemptuous of you if you fail to fight back.

Your goal must be assertiveness, the happy medium between aggression and submission. In fact, standing up without fighting back is surprisingly successful, though with many of us it takes some skill development and some practice to get good enough at it.

Unintentional Threats

In addition to obvious conflict, there are a number of ways to become an accidental or unintentional threat to your boss, and all of them can have the negative consequences that come when you threaten someone in an unequal power relationship.

You will be perceived as a threat (or be one) if you are seen as smarter, more of a go-getter, better connected, or more able than your boss—or if you are seen as seeing yourself as those things. Yet, those elements are clearly positive to the organization as a whole, and equally clearly associated with personal career advancement. How do you resolve this?

- First, remember that the threat comes in the comparison, not in the underlying element. Being smart is good; *smarter* than your boss is bad.
- Second, avoid invidious comparison by building up your boss, not by tearing yourself down. The more successful and able your boss, the more successful and able you can be without becoming a threat.
- Third, use the "goodmouthing" technique to show your full support for your boss at all times.

If these are insufficient to bring the perception of threat under control, the remaining strategy is to avoid any show of ego or self-promotion about your gifts. This won't necessarily solve the entire problem, but it will keep your reputation intact and may take pressure off you.

QUICK TIP SELF-ASSESSMENT

1. Are there any ways in which I am, or could be perceived to be, a threat to my boss?

   _____

   _____

   _____

2. To what extent does my behavior or attitude support that perception? What are the consequences?

    _____

    _____

    _____

3. How can I lower or eliminate any perceived threat while still appearing to be a positive and upwardly mobile professional?

    _____

    _____

    _____

Chapter

18

Accept Responsibility

T he comic-book character Spider-Man once observed, "With great power comes great responsibility."[22] Responsibility and accountability are one of the chief ingredients in management, but they come with a risk: You are responsible for success and also failure.

Command Responsibility for Failure—and Success

Part of your boss's role is to put limits on your responsibility as well as your authority. Like the navy captain who is responsible for the ship running aground even though he or she was not actually even on the bridge at the time, your boss is responsible and accountable for your failures, even if he or she had nothing directly to do with them. This is one reason why bosses are also entitled to claim responsibility for your successes, even if they had nothing directly to do with those, either.

It's important to share the credit, but it's important as well to take the blame when it's appropriate. Legendary football coach Paul "Bear" Bryant put it this way: "If anything goes bad, I did it. If anything goes semigood, then we did it. If anything goes real good, then you did it. That's all it takes to get people to win football games."

22. Lee, Stan, and Steve Ditko. "Spider-Man!" *Amazing Fantasy*, Issue 15, August 1962, p. 11.

Standing Up

Show your support for your boss by standing up to share in the responsibility when things go wrong. Emphasize your role in it. Don't fight, however, when your boss stands up to take the lion's share of the blame or the credit; that's appropriate.

In 1864, General Ulysses S. Grant ordered a cipher operator to turn over the secret key for encoding and decoding messages to a member of his own staff, so he could keep sending and receiving encrypted messages. The operator protested that he was under War Department orders not to give the key to anybody—even Grant. "I told him that if he did not [give me the key] he would most certainly be punished," Grant said. When he returned, he found that the operator had been severely reprimanded and relieved of duty. Grant contacted the secretary of war and informed him that it was his doing, "that they would have to punish me if they punished anybody."[23]

What if your boss dodges responsibility and leaves you holding the sack? Stand up and accept responsibility fully, even if it's not 100 percent yours. You may get into short-term trouble, but you'll find that your reputation for integrity is enhanced. And the truth has a way of emerging in the long run.

QUICK TIP SELF-ASSESSMENT

1. What level of responsibility do I have for project failures?

    _____

    _____

2. What are the consequences of failure?

    _____

    _____

3. How can I better take responsibility for my work?

    _____

    _____

23. Kaltman, Al. Op. cit., p. 133.

Chapter

19

Prepare for Your Meetings

There are various fake management cartoons and memoranda that circle the globe on photocopy machines. No one knows who creates them, but they become part of the hidden communication network inside the organization. Each reveals some frustrating truth about organizational life. In fact, you can learn a lot about the mental health of any organization by wandering the halls and reading the cartoons people post on walls. Often, they are cries for help, funny precisely because they identify the level of frustration and sometimes despair felt by the posting employees.

There's a famous example on the next page. If it describes the meeting culture in your organization, you've got trouble.

You may very well have many bad meetings. But how do bad meetings—or the cure for bad meetings—relate to managing up? In fact, your skill in running, facilitating, or streamlining a meeting can have a disproportionate influence on how you are perceived in the organization, and on your success in getting your goals accomplished.

The Cost of Bad Meetings

If six people have an average salary of $50,000 and they spend even two hours a week in meetings (it would be remarkable if they did not spend more), that amounts to $15,000 a year in direct salary

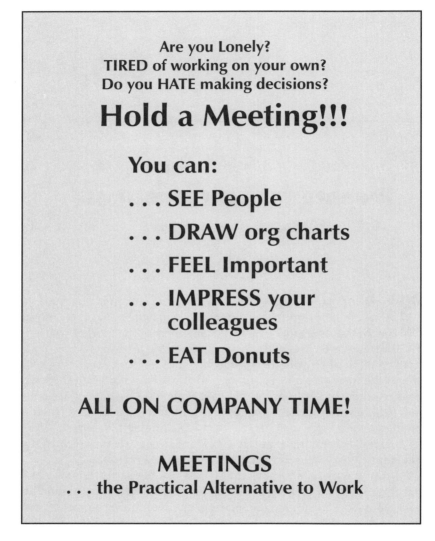

Are you Lonely?
TIRED of working on your own?
Do you HATE making decisions?

Hold a Meeting!!!

You can:

... SEE People

... DRAW org charts

... FEEL Important

... IMPRESS your
    colleagues

... EAT Donuts

ALL ON COMPANY TIME!

MEETINGS
... the Practical Alternative to Work

costs! By the time you add in amounts for overhead, preparation time, materials, room, travel, and—above all—the cost of what people *aren't* doing when they are in a meeting, you'll see there's a major obstacle to productivity right here.

It's worth a few minutes to calculate the actual cost per hour of running a simple staff meeting in your department. Take the annual salaries of the participants (or a good guess) and divide by 2,080 (or just 2,000 so you can do it in your head) to get an hourly wage. If your organization normally calculates overhead costs for employees (costs of benefits, etc.), add in that percentage. Then consider "hard costs" (facility, doughnuts, etc.), and finally figure the work interruption cost, and you'll find that meetings are one of the biggest cost items you have.

It's obvious that bad meetings are wasteful and unproductive, but exactly why are they an important element in successfully managing up? There are several reasons:

- Meetings are the common ground of office communication. How you behave and deal in the context of a meeting has a strong impact on your overall reputation and acceptance.
- Meetings are where major decisions are made or ratified. To be a "player," you have to be part of the right meetings and have the right point of view.
- Meetings, regardless of their other purposes, are also about relationship building, and those relationships affect every other element of your work.

Running Good Meetings

Remember that "bad" is the natural state of meetings. Unless you or someone else takes the steps needed for a good meeting, the meeting will certainly degenerate into complaining, socializing, or argument. Good meetings don't happen by accident, but bad ones do.

What's most interesting is that the secrets of holding a good meeting or being a good meeting participant are hardly secret. Everyone has heard over and over that you should always have an agenda for a meeting. Nevertheless, how many meetings in your organization are held without agendas? The problem is not that people don't know what to do; it's that they don't do it. Why? One reason is that it takes some advance work, and many people feel too rushed to do it. Another reason is that there are some payoffs from running a bad meeting, such as being able to monopolize the discussion, or drag the meeting to your own agenda, not the group's.

One simple way to improve your reputation, effectiveness, and relationships in an organization is to be one of the people who know how to run top-notch meetings—and do so. Among the fringe benefits is that when you are a participant in a meeting, the meeting leader is likely to behave better than he or she might if you were not there.

Your Boss as a "Problem" Meeting Leader or Participant

What if the meeting leader is your boss, and your boss runs bad meetings? First, consider using the Negative Feedback Model to build some assertive communication on the subject. Perhaps your boss doesn't have the necessary skills. Perhaps your boss doesn't know how bad the meetings really are. Your boss may not know that he or she rambles, dominates, or otherwise behaves badly. That's surprising, perhaps, but people are often unaware of the foibles and irritating behavior that may dramatically affect those around them.

An important managing-up skill is providing support to a less-than-effective meeting leader to help him or her achieve desired results. One way is to volunteer to do the necessary preparatory work. For example, you might offer to draft and distribute the agenda—checking, of course, with your boss to make sure that the agenda reflects his or her priorities, not your own.

You might discuss the problem of bad meetings as a general topic, not a specific reflection on the competence (or lack of competence) of any specific individual. It's usually the case that a bad meeting isn't exclusively the fault of the meeting leader; others probably contribute as well. By turning it into a group problem rather than an individual failure, you may have more success in getting the necessary changes.

Finally, you can work on the subtle skill of influencing through your own communication. For example, if the meeting goes off topic, don't challenge directly. Instead, ask an innocent question. "I'm sorry, but I'm getting confused here. How exactly does this relate to the agenda item?"

There aren't many real secrets to holding a good meeting. The obstacle is not lack of knowledge; in most cases, it's lack of will. Work at becoming a "meeting superstar"—a professional who makes every meeting he or she attends of real productive benefit to the organization—and you'll discover enhanced power and influence throughout the organization.

MAKING MEETINGS WORK

1. What do I see as the most common problem areas in meetings?

   Leadership problems _____

   Too many/wrong participants _____

   Participant behaviors _____

   Poor procedures _____

   Lack of purpose _____

   Timing issues _____

2. In what ways do I contribute to problems with meetings?

   _____

   _____

   _____

3. What proactive steps could I take to improve the quality of meetings?

   _____

   _____

   _____

4. What obstacles exist to making those changes?

   _____

   _____

   _____

Chapter
20

Build an Appropriate
Personal Relationship

The whole concept of "work friends" is difficult for many people. Perhaps it's better to think of your office mates more like family than friends, in the spirit of the old saying, "You can choose your friends, but you can't choose your family."

"Remember that nobody at work likes you," said Marilyn Moats Kennedy, "and nobody at work dislikes you, either."[24] She observes that everyone at work wears a "work mask," and that's not a bad thing. Your work mask consists partly of who you are, but also consists of your job title, your hierarchical position, and your level of authority. Your work mask isn't completely your own choice. Everyone who's ever become a manager over people who were once your peers experiences the moment when a friend (or sometimes an ex-friend) comes to you and says, "Ever since you became a supervisor, you've changed."

You may protest, "No, I haven't!" But you have. Authority colors and complicates relationships. Not all the changes in how you are perceived by others are of your own making. There are some in every organization who have an innate problem with authority, which in certain cases may go back to their childhood. Yet when you

24. Kennedy, Marilyn Moats. Op. cit. Audiotape.

occupy an authority position, you take the brunt of those unresolved problems. Similarly, it's hard for us sometimes to conquer all of these issues in terms of how we react and deal with the authority figures in our own lives. Sometimes managing up means dealing with your own personal baggage as well as with whatever personality deficiencies you perceive in those who outrank you.

Of course, none of this means that you can't have some real friendships at work, with your boss or with other managers, or even that all your office friendships are completely insincere. It's obvious that you do bring elements of your true self to the job environment, though some bring more than others. But you aren't and can't be completely your true self at work. You must, in part, be your role, and that's not necessarily hypocritical or phony.

For example, if you're a manager, you may have to discipline or even fire subordinates. That's not a friendly action, and you might well put up with worse behavior from friends than from fellow workers. It's a professional action, and it's part of what you have to think about when you determine your approach to friendship situations at work—especially friendships with your boss or other senior managers.

How personal should your relationship with your boss become? It's impossible to keep a relationship totally on a nonpersonal level when two human beings are involved, but any relationship-building strategy contains risks and concerns.

Focus on the difference between being "friendly" and being "friends." Friendly behavior is positive, cheerful, courteous, interested behavior that need not be restricted to people who are actually your friends. Friendly behavior is showing that you are aware of and have concern for someone else as a human being. Stay aware of personal relationships and how they interact with professional relationships. You may select a variety of strategies, all of which may be perfectly legitimate, but you don't ever want to be unaware of the significance others may read into them.

In the same way the savvy professional quickly learns that office parties aren't parties, make sure you are aware that office friendships aren't friendships, except in rare cases. The proof is when you think about your previous jobs. How many of those people do you still see? Don't be upset that they're not calling you; you probably aren't calling them, either. Your relationship depended in large part on the shared experience and environment of the workplace, and when that ceases, the relationship quickly evaporates. Your real friends are the ones whose continuing relationship doesn't depend on punching the same time clock.

Being part of the social circle at the office can be a critical part of your professional career. From lunch to after-hour drinks to participation in social outings, from playing golf to going to the gym, a tremendous amount of relationship building goes on in the informal organizational environment. As in so many areas of working in the informal organization, balance is critical.

There are some people who center their social life so much on the office that socializing is the primary motive getting them in the door. Work is something unpleasant that interferes with their real goals at the office. Of course, once someone's been identified as belonging to that group, his or her promotion potential is severely hampered. At the other extreme is the person who participates purely for professional gain, gauging every casual interaction based on career advantage. That's no good, either. Do try to have fun, and as serious as the issue of friendship at the office is, not every part of it ought to be calculated for maximum advantage. That strategy is ultimately self-defeating, too.

That leads to the issue of what constitutes an appropriate personal relationship. Unfortunately, the answer depends on the individual environment, and you can get into trouble or damage yourself by stepping over the invisible lines. Ignorance of the unwritten law is no excuse.

Consider the following issues:

What is the nature of the work itself? If the work is clearly divided into unrelated categories, as in the classic factory worker versus management dynamic, then friendship relations across the boundary are often viewed with suspicion on both sides. Work that is more collaborative across the manager/nonmanager boundary normally has a more permissive attitude about friendships. Again, that doesn't mean you can't have a friendship that falls outside the traditional categories, but you need to be aware of issues and potential fallout.

What is the nature of the organization? Every organization naturally has an organizational culture, and the social constraints of the culture often lag behind changes in the reason for those constraints. IBM is a case in point. It's hard to think of a high-technology company as a "suit-mandatory" culture, but IBM was once well-known for highly rigid and formal dress codes. This demonstrated the professionalism of the organization and helped maintain its public image. Clearly, styles have changed, and the term *suit* is sometimes employed as an insult in certain high-tech environments. It's not surprising, however, that IBM's culture changed more slowly, reacting to rather than leading the way. So, if the organization has had a traditional barrier to "fraternization," even if any reason for the barrier has long since evaporated, don't be surprised if the taboo persists.

Take your cues from your boss's relationships with other subordinates, but be aware that some bosses may work too hard at being your "friend." In the same way that a parent who is too much of a friend can become less of a parent, there are obvious reasons why this can be a problem. For example, a romantic or sexual relationship that might be perfectly acceptable between organizational equals (although it may still be the subject of juicy gossip) can be grounds for a sexual harassment lawsuit if it crosses levels of the hierarchy.

While it may be awkward to keep your distance from a boss who wants to be friends to a degree that you don't share (and that's any form of friendship, not just thinly disguised sexual or romantic overtures), you not only have a right to do so, but it may be strongly in your long-term organizational interests to do so. Remember the difference between being friendly, which is not only nice but often politically necessary, and being friends as a good way to help you draw the line.

Appropriate ways to be "friendly" with your boss include: 1) recognition of shared hobbies and interests (e.g., sports), 2) remembering names and key facts about family members, 3) showing concern for personal problems that your boss chooses to bring into the office, and 4) being a good listener.

Make sure you know your company's culture about giving holiday, birthday, and wedding presents, including the amount to spend and whether you should be part of a group present or do something on your own.

Quick Tip Self-Assessment

1. What personal relationship with my boss is appropriate?

———————————————————————————

———————————————————————————

———————————————————————————

2. What is considered inappropriate in my organization's cul-
    ture?

    _____

    _____

    _____

3. How can I improve or expand an appropriate personal rela-
    tionship with my supervisor?

    _____

    _____

    _____

Chapter

21

Look Like a Professional

Mark Twain once observed, "People often ask me why I always wear these white suits. I have traveled all over this world, and I have noticed one thing: Naked people have little or no influence in society."

Whether the dress code is formal or informal, written or unwritten, there is always a dress code in the office. At a high-tech company where "suit" is a swear word, T-shirt conformity can be every bit as rigid as a bank. Image counts. Clothes aren't just clothes; they're a uniform. They send a message; they're part of your nonverbal communication, whether you like it or not. It's therefore a good idea to look like a professional at all times, realizing that professional dress varies from industry to industry, and occasionally from company to company.

Image is clothing, but it's not only clothing. Consider that your overall demeanor and certain key actions communicate much more widely about who you are and how you wish to be perceived. Try these ideas.

- *Dress the part.* What's the right office wardrobe for your organization? The answer isn't always as simple as the "dress for success" books have it. Besides obvious gender dressing issues, some organizations have informal (but quite rigid) standards that vary by hierarchical level.

As odd as it may seem, exceeding your level by too much can actually backfire. In some organizations, you may find the technical rank and file in T-shirts and jeans; middle management in cartoon-character neckties, chinos, and short-sleeve Oxford shirts; and senior management in suits. If someone in the rank and file starts wearing suits—a two-level jump—he or she is likely to be seen more as an oddball than as a senior executive in the making. Moving from jeans to Dockers, on the other hand, and from T-shirts to dressier shirts, is more likely to make you look promotable.

- *Accessorize.* Fashion consultants emphasize accessories, and they matter. In business, the kind of accessories that matter are a good-quality organizer system, a laptop, a professional-looking briefcase, and other tools of the management trade. Again, look around to see what others use; brand snobbery can be as big here as in any high school clique.

- *Be flexible.* The history of fashion shows that over time, sports clothes turn into formal dressing. The tuxedo jacket was so scandalous when invented that you couldn't get into a good club while wearing one. The contemporary work suit used to be casual weekend garb. Sports coats are considered dressy these days, but the name of the jacket identifies its original purpose. Casual Friday dressing is now standard in many industries, and with clothing stores gearing up new "Casual Friday" departments, we see that this trend is not yet over. But as sports clothes migrate into dress clothes, they must change. We're in the middle of a period of rapid evolutionary change in which it's hard to look up the standards in a book. Watch others in the organization and shop carefully, especially if your taste and skill are limited. When you're not sure how to go, middle-of-the-pack is usually your best choice.

QUICK TIP SELF-ASSESSMENT

1. Do I dress the part for the job I want? What changes could I make?

    _____

    _____

    _____

2. Do I have the right accessories—time management system, briefcase, laptop computer—for my goals?

    _____

    _____

    _____

3. How do I demonstrate that I take my job seriously and am someone to consider for promotion?

    _____

    _____

    _____

Chapter

(22)

Give Credit and
Praise Generously

Nothing is impossible to the person who truly doesn't care who gets the credit. In addition to mastering the skills of giving negative feedback, one of the most powerful tools available to you in advancing your relationship with your boss is to give credit and praise generously.

The funny thing about praising your boss is that praise is a form of feedback. By praising, you help establish that you have a right to provide feedback to your boss, which creates a climate in which it's easier to provide negative feedback when warranted.

Quite a lot of research supports the idea that positive feedback alters behavior more consistently and more reliably than negative feedback. "You get more flies with honey than with vinegar," the saying goes. Here's a true story:

> I had this boss that I just wasn't getting along with. I was fresh out of college; he was a retired Air Force colonel. One day he told me to construct a system to keep track of about 180 file cabinets full of important historical data. I put together a pretty complicated numbering system that did the

job, but was a little overcomplicated—almost Rube Gold-
berg-ish.[25]

He looked at the system, nodded, then suggested a little change that got rid of all the complexity and still did all
the job! I was so impressed that I just blurted out, "That's
really clever."

Now, there was no reason he should really care what
some wet-behind-the-ears civilian kid thought, but the
funny thing was that his whole mood changed. I'm not saying all our problems went away, but the truth is, that compliment really made a difference in our relationship. He
could tell I really meant what I said; that it wasn't just a
brown-nose job.

That's when I learned that everybody, no matter who,
likes an honest compliment.

Positive Reinforcement and Feedback

Motivation theorists from Frederick Herzberg to Ken Blanchard emphasize the importance of positive reinforcement—praise and credit
sharing—in motivating employees. Why assume that your boss is
any different? All human beings like to be recognized for their performance.

Positive feedback must recognize real behavior you'd like to see
more of, such as clear directions, good listening, thoughtfulness,
and effective decisions. Positive feedback shouldn't be mixed: "Gee,
that was a pretty good decision—for once." On the other hand, positive feedback can be given for improvement. "I really appreciate
how your decisions have become much more definite and clear. It
really makes it easier for me to do my work."

Positive feedback and positive reinforcement don't just create a
motivational climate and better relationships; they actively change
behavior. If you would like your boss to behave less often in certain
ways and more often in others, or to change his or her way of behaving in almost any area, try offering positive feedback and reinforcement for the behavior you like, and you'll be surprised at the
impact.

25. Rube Goldberg was a well-known cartoonist whose preposterously
overcomplicated machines made his name synonymous with any compli-
cated, wildly impractical invention. **Source:** Hendrickson, Robert. *QPB Encyclopedia of Word and Phrase Origins.* New York: Facts on File, 1997, p. 581.

One surprise may be in store for you—when you start to concentrate on giving people positive feedback, people often initially regard you with suspicion and defensiveness. Be patient; they'll come to appreciate you sooner or later.

The P-R-A-I-S-E Model

You may be nervous about offering positive feedback and reinforcement to your boss for several reasons. First, you may be afraid that your compliment will be perceived as buttering up or brown nosing. Second, you may worry that your praise may be rejected or turned against you. To avoid these dangers, use the "P-R-A-I-S-E" model:

$$\text{Personally}$$
$$\text{Regularly}$$
$$\text{Assertively}$$
$$\text{Immediately}$$
$$\text{Sincerely}$$
$$\text{Explicitly}$$

Personally. Making your feedback personal means that it should be aimed at the specific individual. Use the person's name. Put warmth and approval in your voice and body language. Smile and use eye contact. Share how the positive behavior affected you, and what resulted from it.

Regularly. Motivation author Barbara Fielder suggests using the "ten-coin" technique to improve your skills at positive feedback. "Place ten coins of any denomination in your right pocket. The ten coins jingling in your pocket will remind you to acknowledge employees. Each time you give an employee a positive comment, praise, or recognition, remove a coin from your right pocket and place it in your left pocket. As your day progresses, you can reach into your left pocket, take out the loose change, and quickly find out how many times you've recognized employees that particular day."[26]

This is a powerful technique. Don't limit its use to employees. Add your boss, other managers, professionals in other departments, colleagues, and coworkers, even family members and friends! Build your skills in positive feedback so you transfer all ten coins from one pocket to the other every single day.

By the way, if you try this, don't be surprised if the first reaction you get is suspicion or even outright hostility. "What are you up to? What do you want?" Many people aren't used to getting positive feedback. Be consistent and persistent. Feedback from people who've used this technique suggests that it may take as many as sixty days before you see results.

Assertively. It may seem odd to use the word *assertively* when it comes to praise, yet many people have trouble being assertive enough to offer positive feedback. The fear that our praise will be rejected or scorned is very common, but you'll find that it doesn't often happen. If it does, remember that first attempts to offer positive feedback aren't always successful; it takes persistence. Remember that you have a right to notice and respond to good behavior, no matter where it occurs. A clear and direct tone of voice adds to the power and value of your praise.

Immediately. "You know that great meeting you ran last year? I've been meaning to tell you how much I appreciated it." Not only is that too late to do any good, it conveys the hidden message that the person you're praising hasn't done anything else in the past year worth praising. Give praise and reinforcement as close as possible to the actual event. The longer you wait, the less effective the praise will be, and the less impact it will have on the person's future behavior.

Sincerely. Have you ever received a phony compliment? If you've ever been the recipient of brown-nosing behavior from your own subordinates, you know that you never confuse it with a sincere compliment. Sincere means that the praise must be honest and truly meant. If you can't think of something honest to say, don't say anything—but look harder next time.

Explicitly. "You know, you do good work." That may be nice to hear, but it tells you nothing about what you actually do that the

26. Fielder, Barbara. *Motivation in the Workplace.* Mission, Kans.: SkillPath Publications, 1996, p. 20.

other person respects, admires, or values. For feedback to have the desired effect, you must praise very specific behaviors in a way that the recipient has no doubt about what actions you are recognizing.

Often overlooked in giving positive feedback is that you can recognize very small yet specific behaviors and get a very big payoff. Just make sure the praise is proportional to the deed: "That memo would make Shakespeare weep! It's utter genius! I've never seen anything like it in my whole life! Not to mention your use of semi-colons—wow!" Clearly, that's excessive. Even if it's a really good memo, you don't need to overdo it. "That memo really got the point across. I heard from Mary in accounting that it really helped in the committee meeting" is much better.

Sharing the Credit Effectively

Who gets credit for the good job? That question can lead to conflict, backbiting, poor morale—and a damaged relationship between you and your boss.

Who gets the credit is an important issue in many organizations, because raises, promotions, and bonuses can be at stake. You may have good, strong reasons for working to get credit for the good work you do, but you must be aware that others (especially your boss) may also have strong reasons for claiming at least a share of the credit.

One good slogan to help you is "credit shared is credit multiplied." This is not only practical, it's usually true. It may well have been your work, your decisions, your creativity, and your efforts that brought the project to its successful conclusion, but you are seldom, if ever, a total "solo act."

In organizations, you are always part of a team. While the quarterback may have made the actual touchdown, without the other players as well as the coaches, he'd have been under a pile of opposing players. It's possible for the quarterback to get credit for making the touchdown, which did require personal skill, while also giving credit to the team as a whole for its contributions to the touchdown. For your long-term success, learn to walk that tightrope between taking credit for your performance (crucial to your advancement) and sharing the credit with those others—especially your boss— who helped make it possible. That kind of "assertive modesty" will add immensely to your influence and effectiveness.

Using Praise Effectively

Use the "ten-coin" technique for two weeks to see how much positive feedback you currently offer:

Sunday	Monday	Tuesday	Wednesday	Thursday	Friday	Saturday
Coins:	Coins:	Coins:	Coins:	Coins:	Coins:	Coins:
Sunday	Monday	Tuesday	Wednesday	Thursday	Friday	Saturday
Coins:	Coins:	Coins:	Coins:	Coins:	Coins:	Coins:

AVERAGE: _____ coins per day

Work for the next two weeks to build your number. Take your average and set that as a minimum goal. Add one coin per week until you're consistently at ten. Keep this up for sixty days, and you'll be amazed!

P-R-A-I-S-E Worksheet for Improving Positive Feedback

List each item in the P-R-A-I-S-E model and how you will deliver it:

Personally   _____

Regularly   _____

Assertively   _____

Immediately   _____

Sincerely   _____

Explicitly   _____

Chapter
23

Stand Up for What You Believe and Need

Personal assertiveness is another threshold skill, like goal setting. Develop the skill and courage to stand up assertively for what is right, what you believe, and what you need. You may not always win, but you will earn respect and credibility.

Planning for Assertiveness

Don't spend excessive time worrying about finding just the right word or phrase to express yourself when you need to be assertive. The right word or phrase may not exist, but even if it does, it's the attitude and body language more than the *mot juste* that gets the point across. Many people profit from some degree of rehearsal or preplanning when they expect to have a potentially difficult situation. The problem is often that you imagine what they will say, but they say something entirely different, throwing you off course. Instead of scripting out what you will say, and then what they will say, focus your planning energy on goals: What do I want to happen? What do I think they want to happen? What strategy is most likely to give me the outcome I want while preserving dignity and face on all sides of the issue?

By focusing on goals and outcomes, rather than verbal tactics and strategies, you'll find it easier to respond assertively in a way that preserves the relationship.

Consideration of Consequences

It's unfortunate but true that the mere fact that you've been assertive doesn't automatically make others nice and reasonable in return. In fact, people can become angry, say harsh things, or perhaps even seek retribution. However, there are several ways you can improve the situation.

First, if you are afraid to be assertive, make a list of the consequences you fear. Write them down on a piece of paper. Then look at your list. For each item, consider the following:

- How likely is it that this consequence will actually occur? The degree of legitimate worry should be related to the likelihood of the consequence.
- How serious is the consequence? Assume it happens. What will the actual effects on you be? Are all the negative aspects internal and emotional, or are at least some of them external and real? Again, the degree of your concern ought to relate to the seriousness of the consequences.
- What can you do to minimize negative effects? Assume the negative consequences occur and that the effects are as serious as they can be. What can you do about them? Are there steps you can take in advance to minimize or eliminate the negative effects? Are there steps you can take after the fact?

In many cases, a good, hard, realistic look at the situation will demonstrate that this is a case of FEAR (False Evidence Appearing Real). When you discover your fears are illusory, it's relatively easy to get them under control.

On the other hand, sometimes you discover that your fears are real, and that a certain course of conduct may well deliver bad results. All the experts and authorities who recommend that you be assertive in cases in which your rights are being challenged would probably agree that being assertive to an armed mugger might be a bad response. In that case, you can consider other alternatives, from giving in to changing your situation.

Nonverbal Communication

Assertive behavior is most often described as being communication behavior—what you say and how you say it. Of course, much of communication, including tone of voice, body language, and other aspects of your presentation, doesn't include the actual words you say.

Demonstrate good eye contact when you're being assertive. Stand up straight. These are skills that improve with practice and success. There are tricks of the trade, too. For example, remember that when it comes to eye contact, most people can't tell whether you're looking them in the eye or not as long as your gaze is steady. Try looking at the bridge of the nose, or an eyebrow, or an upper lip if you're having trouble looking directly into someone's eyes. Practice the technique first in a nonstressful situation, checking to see when someone can tell you're not giving eye contact. Then you'll know it works, and next time you'll appear strong and assertive, even if you really can't look the person in the eye.

You can practice your body language in front of a mirror or by using a video camera. Are you standing straight (or sitting up straight)? Do your hands move as if they had a life of their own, showing nervousness and defensiveness? Does your foot twitch uncontrollably when you're tense? Many people have physical signs—telltales—that can reveal nervousness or defensiveness to others. In addition, some gestures or posture can appear threatening to the other person. People think they're being assertive, and in their language they might well be assertive. But their body language comes across as aggressive. Perception, in such cases, *is* reality. By becoming aware of any physical signs that undercut the message you want to send, you'll discover that over time you can reduce or eliminate them.

Similarly, it's worthwhile to listen to your voice on a tape or video recorder. Hardly anyone likes the sound of his or her own voice, but try to disregard those feelings. Ask yourself, is my voice clear and strong? Do my sentences go up at the end as if they are all questions? Do I have verbal tics, such as "and-uh" or "you know"? Does the sound of my voice reflect the image I want to project? If you detect problems, there are many courses, groups, and self-study programs you can use to help you change.

QUICK TIP SELF-ASSESSMENT

1. Where do I fall on the continuum of passive-assertive-aggressive behavior?

    _____

    _____

    _____

2. Do I have any self-limiting beliefs or fears that move me to the extremes of passive or aggressive behavior?

    _____

    _____

    _____

3. Are there any elements of tone of voice or nonverbal communication that tend to undercut the message I want to send?

    _____

    _____

    _____

4. What steps can I take to be more assertive on a regular basis?

    _____

    _____

    _____

Chapter

(24)

Be Informative, but Not a "Tattletale"

Your boss needs to know about problems and issues that affect the department and the work. Sometimes, those involve the performance of other people. It's difficult sometimes to walk the tightrope of being informative without becoming a tattletale. How do you balance the legitimate needs of your boss to know about work performance issues with the need to avoid a reputation for telling tales?

When Not to Tell

The consequences of being known as a tattletale are serious enough that you should look for alternatives when possible. When there are no good alternatives, you don't have a choice but to do so.

Respect confidences, except in the most extreme circumstances. If someone privately tells you he or she is committing criminal behavior, if someone privately suggests he or she plans to harm himself or herself or others, you have no choice but to violate the confidence; in all other circumstances, keep quiet.

Keep any kind of negative sharing to an absolute minimum. If you don't have to carry negative tales, don't.

Don't volunteer information unnecessarily. Sometimes, the issue is whether you're being pinned down by someone in authority, or whether you're originating the information without it being asked for. Tattling on your boss, for example, is almost always a bad move. But if you're pinned down by someone at a very senior level of management, you may have to say something, and it had better be the truth.

When You Have to Tell

There are clearly situations in which you have no choice. You must tell, and sometimes you have to initiate the conversation. If you find someone stealing, passing confidential information to customers, or engaging in behavior that could make your organization vulnerable to a lawsuit or criminal charges, you have to speak up. Use this checklist:

First, assess the seriousness of the performance situation. Do you need to provide information on this, or can it be safely ignored?

Second, determine if you can act on your own. If someone needs coaching, see if you can provide it. If someone is engaging in sabotage, sometimes simply showing that you're aware of it can bring the problem to a halt without the need to escalate.

Third, assess how it might appear. If you're ratting on a rival, no matter how legitimate, you can expect to have your motives for telling questioned. Do you have anything to gain if that person gets into trouble or is fired? Is there bad blood between you and this person? Have you brought three or four other situations involving that person to your boss's attention already?

Fourth, figure out what your boss would most likely do. If you've brought up similar issues before and your boss hasn't taken action, that should be a hint to let it alone this time—even if you disagree about its importance. (If you keep bringing it up now, that can be construed as a negative judgment about your boss.)

Fifth, consider whether you personally need to bring it up. Is someone else likely to do it? Will it become quickly obvious to your boss? Can you provide the information indirectly, such as in a report or briefing that doesn't involve naming names? Can your boss be induced to see the situation directly?

How to Tell

If you decide you must bring it up, do it in private and make sure you present it in the proper manner. Focus exclusively on the work issues and make sure you deal in specifics, not generalities or negative language. ("He's always late, you know," or "She's messed up again.") Use a "more in sorrow than in anger" tone. Don't recom-

mend a specific action; let your boss decide. Let him or her know
you're uncomfortable bringing it up (assuming you are). Don't follow up with your boss about actions taken. If you discover that
management is well aware of the situation and chooses not to act,
then you need to leave it alone.

When Someone's in the Hot Seat Unfairly

People in power have been known to shift the blame that should
rightly be theirs onto someone of lower power and status. Chain-of-
command issues being very serious, you should think several times
before getting involved, especially if it's not your issue. You may,
for example, be wrong in your assessment, or perhaps there's blame
to go around. What is your proof? If it's just your observation and
you can't substantiate it, you may find yourself getting into trouble
without helping the victim.

Here is one of those times you need the network of contacts
and relationships we've discussed. Talk unofficially to your mentor.
Sometimes you may find that senior management is already aware
of the problem and is laying the groundwork for action. It may not
come soon enough to suit you, but having you go formal about your
complaint may make things worse.

What if it's you who's being unfairly blamed in order to shift
responsibility away from the manager who owns it? The best defense against such a move comes well in advance. Here are five ideas
that will help reduce the likelihood of this happening to you.

- First, the quality of your overall reputation for good work has a
  lot to do with (a) whether others will believe you are being unfairly treated, and (b) whether a manager inclined to shift blame
  will choose you as the target.
- Second, keep a running work diary and thorough files on what
  you do—documentation is your best defense.
- Third, understand that catching some blame is part of many peo-
  ples' job description. You may need to simply accept a certain
  amount of blame, even if it's unfair.
- Fourth, check in with your network contacts regularly, especially
  with those inclined to believe in you and support you.
- Fifth, own up to mistakes you do make honestly and quickly. That
  will help insulate you from unfair accusations.

Quick Tip Self-Assessment

1. Is there a situation involving a coworker my boss needs to know about?

   _____

   _____

   _____

2. Is there an option about whether I must tell my boss?

   _____

   _____

   _____

3. What techniques can I use to minimize the negativity involved?

   _____

   _____

   _____

Chapter
(25)

Build Mentoring and Networking Relationships Throughout the Organization

"**M**entoring" and "networking" have become so overused—and abused—that they are in danger of becoming clichés. It's pretty obvious that for you to be successful and grow, you need to cultivate people in your life at all levels, areas, and interests. It's important to understand the fundamental behaviors and know how to apply them if you are to be truly successful in managing up.

Mentoring

Mentors are people who give you help and advice based on their own position, experience, knowledge, and accomplishments. Mentors can be role models, trainers, and coaches. You need to develop effective, mutually beneficial relationships with people outside your own department and your own chain of command. There are clear benefits to you in developing mentoring relationships, including the development of good role models, emotional support, and a "safe haven" to discuss certain issues and concerns you might feel are inappropriate to bring to your boss—such as problems you're having with your boss.

Mentors also provide coaching, recommendations on skill development and behavior, and a candid assessment of how you're doing without a potentially punitive impact on your next raise, promotion, or bonus. Most important, mentors can help teach you about the hidden reality of organizational life and culture, the invisible lines you can't cross.

Mentors and your boss. While your boss is and must be an essential element in your success within the organization, you must expand your reach and relationships to truly succeed. The trick, of course, is how to develop these relationships without a) threatening your boss or b) appearing to be a brownnoser.

The first issue may be the most difficult, depending on how threatened or vulnerable your boss may feel. In order not to generate feelings of paranoia in your boss, which would certainly be counterproductive, you need to make sure that your boss knows that you are personally loyal to him or her, and that nothing in the outside relationships will be used to undercut that relationship.

In addition, try to make sure that the value you get from mentoring relationships also provides direct benefit and support to your boss. For example, if you discover useful information and insight, pass it on—respecting confidentiality, of course. Remember that there is not a lot of benefit in hogging a mentoring relationship. If your boss is not well-connected in the organization, share your connections. It won't hurt you and it will benefit him or her.

Avoiding brown nosing. The second issue is avoiding appearing to be a brownnoser. It is this problem that has given mentoring somewhat of a bad name. You certainly want advancement, and you are looking for benefits in a mentoring relationship. What does the mentor get out of providing you with help and support? When the relationship is mutually beneficial, the suspicion of brown nosing goes away.

What are the benefits to the mentor in the mentoring process? Consider some of the following:

- It's flattering to be admired, respected, and thought of as a role model.
- One's personal power and influence increases by developing other people.

- The people being mentored can provide the mentor with direct support and effort toward his or her goals.
- The mentor gains access to wider information and different points of view.

Things to avoid. Mentor is often a loaded word, and it's not the best thing to ask someone to be your mentor outright. Instead, ask for help and advice and be prepared to build the relationship over time.

Listen to your mentor. If you receive advice, at a bare minimum you'd better take it seriously. Think about it. If you brush off the advice, be prepared not to get any more. You don't have to take all the advice you're given; some won't fit you, and some may be wrong. But you do have to be appreciative and thankful.

Don't be too obvious, desperate, or needy. As the Albert Brooks character said in the movie *Broadcast News*, "Wouldn't this be a wonderful world if being depressed and needy made us *more* attractive?"

When you have someone willing to mentor you, don't delay or drag your feet. If you don't appear willing and eager for help, the desire to help goes way down.

Ideally, you want to develop a network of contacts, mentors, and resources, not just one.

Networking

Networking is about maximizing the people resources available to you, the contacts, knowledge, insights, and relationships that open doors and leverage your own abilities.

As with the word *mentoring,* try to avoid actually using the word *networking* to describe what you do, because the connotation for many people has become negative and manipulative. Think of it as relationship building, talking with people, getting to know the people in your organization, learning about the work of different departments. All of these are clearly legitimate, positive actions that not only increase your value, but also provide benefits for the people being "networked."

Building a robust and wide network of relationships is one of the best tools you can develop, and it's well worth the work and effort. Most good job opportunities are filled through contacts and contacts of contacts. A significant part of your ability to get things done is a function of your network, your opportunity to work with and through others.

You don't want to make networking about using other people. Offer information, support, and help to others in the process. Some people consider the concept "you scratch my back, I scratch yours" to be ethically questionable. But look at it this way: If you scratch my back and I scratch yours, two of us don't itch any more. That's good. When the information and support we trade in networking is legitimate, then trading is positive and ethically appropriate. Only if you're trading confidences or inappropriate favors does an ethical issue arise.

Your ultimate power and influence in the organization, from bottom to top, depends on the range of contacts and relationships you have, both in the organization itself and in the overall industry in which you work. Here are some tips for building an effective network in a principled fashion:

- Go to lunch with different people on a regular basis.
- Ask questions to get to know the person as an individual as well as questions to understand his or her role in the organization.
- Participate in office parties, picnics, sports teams, and other informal groups. This is work, not just fun.
- Make sure you use proper business and communications etiquette.
- Absolutely respect any and all confidences shared with you.
- Follow through on any promises you make. If you can't keep your promise, at a minimum go back to the person and explain the situation.
- Listen and consider the advice you get, whether or not you eventually follow it.
- Join associations, trade groups, and professional societies in your field to expand your relationships in other organizations.
- Volunteer for committees and project groups that give you cross-departmental contacts.

Make networking and relationship building a habit. Set yourself a personal goal of at least one new contact each week. Set aside regular time to call and follow up on your relationships, but don't pester people.

As in the case of mentoring, make sure you use the information and support to help achieve your boss's goals; don't let it appear to be a threat—actual or even potential.

MENTORING AND NETWORKING

1. Make a list of current contacts in other departments in your organization.

    _____

    _____

    _____

2. Who are the "power players" with whom you should build relationships?

    _____

    _____

    _____

3. What activities, both professional and personal, are these people involved in?

    _____

    _____

    _____

4. What would I like to get from networking and mentoring relationships?

    _____

    _____

    _____

5. What can I offer—in terms of support, help, and information—to my networking and mentoring relationships?

    _____

    _____

    _____

Chapter

26

Listen

Good listening skills are essential to the art of managing up. Management expert Norma Carr-Ruffino observes, "Saying the right things to the right people at the right time requires good listening skills. . . . The ability to communicate empathy, encouragement, and acceptance of the speaker depends mainly on what you *don't* say."[27] It's very common for people to think that in a conversation the talker is active and the listener is passive. It's also dead wrong. Listening—active listening—communicates as powerfully as anything you say. Active listening means concentrating on the other person, showing that you are listening, and verifying that you're correctly receiving the message.

The following elements of active listening are crucial to having a successful relationship with your boss:

- *Listening for content.* Use paraphrasing to make sure you receive and understand the messages you're given, whether orders or information. "Let me make sure I understand you correctly. If I understand, what you said was [paraphrase]."
- *Listening for emotional context.* How does the speaker feel about what is being discussed? Listen for tonal qualities, emotional

27. Carr-Ruffino, Norma. *The Promotable Woman.* 2d ed. Belmont, Calif.: Wadsworth, 1993, p. 221.

statements, and exaggerations that provide clues to the emotional content of the message.

- *Listening for priority.* What cues are being given that help assess the priority of the message? Is it important? How does it compare to other messages?
- *Listening for relationship.* Remember that the simple act of listening automatically relieves stress and builds relationships. It's one of the quickest and easiest ways to show support.

It's not enough to listen; you must look like you're listening. Be aware of body language and eye contact that shows you are really paying attention. Body language listening cues involve such things as leaning forward, polite interjections ("Really?" "Interesting." "No kidding!"), head nodding, and the like. Eye contact should be regular, but avoid staring.

It's not rude to take notes while listening. In fact, it shows real interest, while helping you keep a good record of what's being said. Finally, when you have to cut someone off (you've got to get back to work), always validate the other person by saying something like, "I really want to hear what you have to say; I have to leave now." Avoid the word *but* before the second clause; it tends to invalidate in the hearer's mind everything that comes before the "but." Suggest a follow-up meeting or another time to hear the rest of the story.

Quick Tip Self-Assessment

1. What are my current listening strengths?

   _____

   _____

2. What are my current listening weaknesses?

   _____

   _____

3. How can I improve my listening ability?

   _____

   _____

Chapter

27

Tolerate Some Bad Moods

Y ou say "Good morning" as your boss passes you in the hall, but what you get is a grump and semisnarl as your boss strides past you as if you don't even exist. It's hard not to wonder what you've done wrong, or whether you're in some sort of trouble.

No one likes to be mistreated or abused, but you need to make sure you know the difference between a random, nonpersonal bad mood and actual abuse. Don't hold your boss to inhuman standards of perfection, assuming that he or she is not entitled to be grumpy or negative.

Dealing With Bad Moods

First, make sure you're aware of the behavioral cues that tell you when your boss is in a bad mood, remembering that bad moods can come from situations totally outside work. Even when the bad moods are work related, they aren't necessarily about you.

Second, don't escalate the bad mood unnecessarily. Ask yourself what part of your business can wait until later, especially unpleasant business.

Third, ask yourself what you can do proactively, either professionally (get something done without bothering your boss, or solve a problem on your own) or personally (saying something cheerful or sharing a good joke), depending on the nature of your relationship.

Bad Moods vs. Abuse

There is clearly a behavior level at which bad moods become abusive behavior. It's helpful to distinguish between a one-time incident in which someone loses his or her temper and says things that he or she later regrets, and someone whose general coping style involves anger, temper, and belittling others. The latter is clearly more serious.

Although abusive behavior takes various forms, it tends to have at least some of these characteristics: The behavior is chronic, attacks you as a person, tends to generalize ("you always do this"), is public, or is disproportionate to any specific offense you may have committed. Unfortunately, however, abusive behavior is not per se illegal. To be illegal, the abuse must be targeted at you because of your sex, race, creed, or ethnicity, or must involve slurs or other remarks concerning your membership in a protected group. For illegal behavior, keep good notes and talk to an attorney who specializes in such matters.

A number of books and resources can help you learn how to deal with difficult people, including how to deal with situations in which the other person outranks you and may have the power to do you damage. Obviously, the second situation is more difficult for anyone to handle.

Try some of the following ideas:

- Study the abusive behavior to understand it. Is it really directed at you, or are you simply the convenient victim?
- Study the patterns and timing of the behavior. Is it associated with some other situation that might be easier for you to control?
- Practice an assertive response—neither aggressive nor submissive—to send the message that the abusive behavior isn't working on you. It's unfortunate, but, as many of us learned in elementary school, if you react to the behavior, you get more of it. The less you seem to react to the behavior, the less of it you'll tend to get.
- Determine if anyone can help, especially if the behavior slides across the line into areas where you are entitled to legal protection. Look for people who are dealing successfully with the behavior, if others are being subjected to it as well, and try to use their techniques if possible.
- Don't overreact. It may be true that the behavior is 90 percent your boss's doing and only 10 percent your own contribution. If you protest, you'll find that your minor contribution becomes inflated. It's unfair that the lower-ranked person will be held to a higher standard, but that is what most commonly happens.

QUICK TIP SELF-ASSESSMENT

1. What are the bad mood tip-offs for my boss?

    _____

    _____

    _____

2. What are the strategies most likely to work with my bad-mood boss?

    _____

    _____

    _____

3. What proactive steps can I take to get the work done and keep problems off my boss's desk?

    _____

    _____

    _____

Chapter

28

Demonstrate Total Loyalty and Respect the Chain of Command

You can't manage your boss—as opposed to manipulating your boss—without your boss's cooperation. The truth is that many bosses actively welcome being managed. In supervisory seminars, when managers are asked, "How many of you have at least one employee who really knows how to manage you?" quite a few hands go up. When the follow-up question, "How many of you really appreciate it?" is asked, most of the hands stay up.

Why would a boss *want* to be managed by a subordinate? Some of the answers include:

- "It makes my job a lot easier when I know my staff is looking out for me."
- "My subordinate really knows where I'm weak and gives me the support I need."
- "Sometimes I'm pretty disorganized, and my staff member keeps me straight."
- "I like knowing that there's at least one person on the team who'll give me a straight answer—whether or not I want to hear it."

Managers value being "managed" by their staff for all the reasons they know they need to provide management to their staff. When someone is being managed effectively, he or she becomes more focused and more productive. He or she receives the feedback and developmental support that everyone needs at some level and at some time.

Managers who don't like being managed by their staff have their reasons too:

- "I don't like being manipulated."
- "My subordinate uses me to get his or her own way."
- "I feel patronized and that my authority is being eroded."

These are also reactions that some subordinates have to their managers. Although good management is appreciated and valued, bad management is resented, regardless of whether the management is up or down.

Focus on the essential differences between a "managing" relationship and a "manipulating" relationship, and you'll find yourself in the first set of reactions, not the second.

Total Loyalty

The key characteristic you must develop to make your managing up a productive and mutually beneficial experience for your boss is the concept of total loyalty. A good manager is loyal to you as a subordinate, wanting you to succeed for your own sake, for the sake of the department and organization, and also for the sake of your boss. When you feel that you are supported and valued, it's easier to take—and even welcome—feedback and suggestions for change and growth. Demonstrate the same behavior upward that you appreciate and value downward.

Promotable Women author Norma Carr-Ruffino observes that perhaps the best way to build a relationship with your boss based on loyalty and trust is to be alert to opportunities to make your boss look good, especially to his or her bosses.[28] She also recommends that you give the boss credit for changes you make, but be sure to file away memos documenting your role for use in promotion or raise negotiations, and consider documenting your boss's accomplishments as well as your own.

Being a team player means believing, and acting as if you believe, that your success and achievement is only possible as part of

28. Carr-Ruffino, Norma. Op. cit., p. 269.

a team—a team led by your boss. You can still gain legitimate credit for your activities, but you'll have much better luck when your successes aren't seen as somehow taking away from your boss.

This emphasis on loyalty and team player behavior underlies many of the other recommendations in this book. Some of the recommended strategies won't work at all if loyalty isn't there. All of the rest of them will be enhanced and far more effective if done with loyalty. Your goal is to manage your boss, not manage "around" your boss.

What if yours is a problem boss? While you'll learn some specific techniques in a later chapter, you should remember that changing or coping with a problem boss is made much easier if that boss feels you have loyalty and team spirit at base.

No matter what the situation, you must find a way to demonstrate loyalty to your boss as part of your strategy for success.

Understanding and Respecting the Chain of Command

The chain of command is one of management's many borrowings from the military. In a traditional organization (or military unit), each person is responsible to one immediate supervisor, and that supervisor is in turn responsible to a higher-level supervisor or manager, and so on to the top of the organization. Lines of authority are clear in this type of structure.

You may work in a matrix management structure instead of a traditional hierarchical structure. In matrix management, people are grouped together for a specific project in ways that bypass the traditional chain of command. This may be a temporary situation, or it may be a permanent management philosophy. You should be aware that even in a matrix or team structure there is still a chain of command, although it may be more general and sometimes unofficial in nature.

Violating the chain of command means to bypass one or more intermediate levels of supervision to get job assignments or decisions from a higher level. Although it may be tempting as a short-run strategy, especially if you're not getting the support you need or want from your immediate boss, this behavior has several drawbacks:

- It can result in confusion, bad decisions or mistakes, because each level of the chain has certain information and goals to achieve. Bypassing the chain cuts that information out of the process.

- It smacks of a child trying to corner one parent or the other alone to get a favorable decision after the other parent has already said "no."
- It shows lack of loyalty to your own supervisor, which not only harms that relationship, but also raises questions about you in the minds of those in higher levels of management.
- It shows lack of understanding about the organizational structure, which also raises questions about you in the minds of others.

When You're Not Violating the Chain of Command

You're not violating the chain of command if you have permission or clearance from lower levels to move upward in the chain. You're still responsible for keeping those in the middle fully informed.

You're not violating the chain of command if you've been assigned to a project, committee, or other special work with someone several levels above you in the chain, as long as your immediate supervisor was properly informed and consulted.

You're not violating the chain of command if you have developed mentoring and networking relationships with people in higher management levels as long as you don't use those relationships to reverse your boss's decisions, get job assignments without your boss's approval, or keep your boss in the dark about those relationships.

When You Are Violating the Chain of Command

You *are* violating the chain of command if you are approached by someone higher in management who gives you a job assignment or decision and if you don't either ask the manager to clear it with your boss or, at an absolute minimum, personally clear it with your boss at the earliest practical moment. That doesn't mean you should refuse the assignment or be uncooperative with the senior person. He or she is also violating the chain of command, and it's still negative behavior even though he or she has the power to do so. Don't compound the mistake by keeping your boss out of the loop.

Note that if your boss feels bypassed by his or her own boss, feelings of paranoia and persecution may result. It is obviously more difficult for your boss to confront or change the behavior of his or her own superior (especially if your boss hasn't fully mastered his or her own managing up skills), so you may find yourself bearing the brunt of your boss's resentment. Depending on your relationship with the senior person, asking him or her to check with your boss may be a supportive and practical thing to do.

BUILDING TRUST AND SHOWING LOYALTY

1. Does my boss currently feel that I am loyal and supportive of him or her?

   Yes _____   No _____

2. What behaviors and actions do I currently perform that show loyalty and "team player" behaviors?

   _____

   _____

   _____

3. What behaviors and actions do I currently perform that might show lack of loyalty and support?

   _____

   _____

   _____

4. Are there any ways in which I have violated the chain of command or given my boss the feeling that I have violated the chain of command (including relationships with higher-ups and job assignments received but not sought out)?

   _____

   _____

   _____

5. How could I better show my loyalty and support?

   _____

   _____

   _____

Chapter

29

Learn to Handle Criticism

While giving criticism and negative feedback is an essential characteristic of managing up, learning how to accept it yourself is equally important. Assertiveness expert Madelyn Burley-Allen observes, "Being able to handle criticism is a definite step toward being fully in charge of yourself. Because criticism often includes blame and judgment, it may lead to feeling victimized and defensive. The problem with defensive behavior is that it cuts the other person off, which usually intensifies the situation."[29]

If you are particularly sensitive to criticism—and at some level, who isn't?—you will find it worthwhile to work at desensitizing yourself. Criticism, both competently and incompetently provided, is a common ingredient in organizational life, and we all get our share.

A good tool to minimize the emotional impact of criticism is to be the instigator, not merely the recipient. Arrange regular opportunities to get feedback about your performance from your boss, and specifically ask for negative feedback. "Are there any areas or situations in which you would like to see me improve or change or handle something differently next time?" When you ask for negative feedback, it will usually be delivered with less force and emotion than when someone is upset because of a mistake. Because you are being proactive, the situation will end up feeling less negative than otherwise.

29. Burley-Allen, Madelyn. *Managing Assertively: How to Improve Your People Skills.* New York: John Wiley & Sons, 1983, p. 142.

Another strategy is recommended by noted self-esteem expert Jack Canfield. He suggests you keep a Victory Log of all your everyday successes, no matter how small. Most of us remember our failures much more vividly than our successes. When negative criticism is painful, or you're having fears about your ability to handle a new situation, read your Victory Log to see how well you've done in the past. By balancing negative emotion with positive, you'll find yourself able to put the criticism into perspective.[30]

Don't overlook your potential opportunity to change the criticism and feedback style of a particularly negative boss. While it's difficult, it's seldom as impossible or out of the question as most people assume. First, consider using the Negative Feedback Model (Chapter 16) to structure your approach. Making sure you use behavioral rather than judgmental language, actually talk to your boss about his or her style of feedback. Remember that giving poor feedback actually hurts your boss's ability to get what he or she wants, and changing a style may be highly beneficial to your boss. There are positive reasons for change, and when you focus on them, you can often get good results.

QUICK TIP SELF-ASSESSMENT

1. In what areas am I aware of my need to improve?

    _____

    _____

2. How can I lower my own defensiveness or resentment when I am criticized?

    _____

    _____

3. Could I request some negative feedback in order to improve myself in key areas?

    _____

    _____

30. Canfield, Jack. *How to Build High Self-Esteem.* Audiotape. Chicago: Nightingale-Conant, 1989, side 7.

Chapter

Get Organized

ix out of ten professionals pick up the same piece of paper on their desk as many as twenty-one times.[31] Disorganization not only destroys efficiency and productivity, but also has relationship implications that affect your ability to manage up.

If You Have a Problem

If you're one of the "organizationally challenged," remember that perfection isn't necessary. A spotless desk isn't vital to your success, only one clean enough to enable you to work effectively. The old housework euphemism about having a lived-in look can apply to your office environment as well.

Getting Started

For many people, getting started is the hardest part. Here's a good first step that will deliver immediate benefits.

Take half a Saturday to organize your office. Don't follow someone's organizational scheme blindly: Your office is your productivity tool and it needs to be oriented to your own style and work habits. Make sure the items you need regularly are within your reach. That includes not only basics like staplers, pens, and paper clips, but also frequently used files and books.

31. Study performed by Fortino & Associates, reported in the *Wall Street Journal*, 2 May 1989, and cited in Temme, Jim. *Productivity Power*. Mission, Kans.: SkillPath Publications, 1993, p. 107.

Set up project files for major projects, and build a tickler file to store information you'll need in the next month. (A tickler file has different folders or pockets for each day in a month, or sometimes each month in a year. It's a combination time machine and file cabinet.)

Susan Silver's book *Organized to Be the Best!* lists (and reviews) the myriad tools that are made and sold to help you get organized. In addition to studying what's available, try these two tricks: First, spend an hour wandering the aisles of a big office supply store, or poring through a catalog. You'll be amazed at the tools available. Don't go crazy in buying new tools; think first. Second, keep an eye out for the good organizational tricks others around you are practicing. If you find an idea that works for you, use it.

How to *Really* Handle Pieces of Paper Only Once

Almost everyone has heard over and over again the rule that you should pick up each paper on your desk only once, but in practice that's a tough rule to follow. Instead, try this tip: Put a check mark on each paper as you pick it up. If you pick it up a second time without having acted, put a second check mark on it, and so on. You'll be amazed at how quickly the reinforcement of seeing those check marks reduces your unnecessary paper handling!

QUICK TIP SELF-ASSESSMENT

1. What are my major organizational problems and weaknesses?

   _____

   _____

2. Are there specific tools I need to stay on top of the situation?

   _____

   _____

3. Are there references, seminars, or systems I can use to get myself better organized?

   _____

   _____

Chapter

31

Limit the "Great Ideas" and Sell Them Effectively

In *The First-Time Supervisor's Survival Guide*, George Fuller makes this important observation: "The natural inclination of someone new is to try to impress the boss. This is often interpreted to mean making suggestions and the like which will show the boss how smart you are. Surprisingly, this isn't the best or brightest way to win the admiration of a boss. What every boss looks for is a smooth and efficient operation that gets the job done with a minimum of problems—in short, as few headaches as possible."[32]

Does this mean that you shouldn't identify problems, come up with creative solutions, and be an agent for change within your department? Of course not. Those behaviors are valuable and appropriate. Proposing your ideas, selling them, and making them a reality is always something you do upward in an organization: It's a key part of managing up. Yet, mastering this skill is one of the most difficult challenges you are likely to face.

Just remember that your credibility and power to make these changes must be earned. It's not enough to be right that a proposed change is desirable; you have to earn the right to make the sugges-

32. Fuller, George. *The First-Time Supervisor's Survival Guide*. Englewood Cliffs, N.J.: Prentice Hall, 1995, p. 32.

tion in the first place, and you do that through demonstrating that you're on top of the situation just the way it is. Notice that the strategy for making change work is to combine the need for total loyalty with our first suggestion: Do good work.

There are three problems with recommending major changes right off the bat. First, you probably don't know what you're talking about. If the problem and its solution look so obvious, yet no one has taken action, perhaps there's a deeper level you should know about before you get started. Second, nobody likes a know-it-all. If your style is abrasive, you'll get off on the wrong foot with everyone. Third, you're trying to make your boss look like an idiot, which is an example of the famous CLM, or Career Limiting Move.

This dilemma—that being right isn't usually enough to achieve change—is a source of never-ending frustration for a number of people. You'll notice them in every organization, hard at work selling their ideas, becoming increasingly disenchanted and negative about management, and never understanding that their own performance and credibility dramatically affects their ability to achieve desired change. Don't let yourself become one of these people. You can avoid that situation by mastering the basics and building from there.

Given that one goal of learning to manage up is to achieve organizational growth and change in the directions you believe are right, how can you successfully sell your ideas?

Strategies for Selling Your Ideas

As you become familiar with the work in an organization, and especially when you get a promotion or are put in a new position, you naturally tend to identify problems and come up with ideas about how the work processes can be improved. It's frustrating when you don't seem to be able to get your boss and others in management to recognize the problem or the value of your solution.

If you're having problems selling your ideas and recommendations to management, look at some key elements that may be involved.

1. *Do you understand the situation sufficiently?* One characteristic of the chain of command is that some information and perspective is only available at certain levels. Here's a true story:

> I was working for a consumer products manufacturer that was really popular with kids. They would come to our company and want to buy stuff from us, but we didn't sell directly to consumers.

I thought, "Hey, we have a warehouse full of stuff, a receptionist out front, and kids who want to give us money!" So I proposed to my boss that we put some products in a cabinet in the lobby and have the receptionist take the money when kids wanted to buy. Not a major source of income, but no real cost. I thought it was pretty much a no-brainer.

My boss liked the idea, and he said he'd bring it up with the senior staff. But when he came back, he said, "Your idea really made the head of accounting go ballistic. I don't know what his problem is, but he's mad at you. Stay out of his way."

Of course, I immediately went to see the head of accounting to find out what the problem was. He said, "The problem with your idea is you didn't figure the impact it had on us. We don't charge sales tax, we don't take credit cards . . . we're not a retailer. Do you have any idea of what we'd have to go through to set up that system to make it work? It's just not worth it."

I apologized, of course—and I got a free lesson in finance in the bargain.

Some ideas seem like mere common sense at first, but there may be factors elsewhere in the organization that make them unworkable. Pushing that kind of idea makes you look naive at best, thoughtless and ill-prepared at worst. The normal human temptation is to look for reasons that support your great idea. Instead, look for reasons your idea might be wrong or inappropriate before you advocate it publicly. Another benefit in having a network and mentors is that you have some people who'll tell you what may be wrong with your proposals before you embarrass yourself or get into trouble.

2. *Whose oxen might be gored?* Here's another true cautionary tale:

I found a way to put in some automation that would allow us to cut twenty positions, saving hundreds of thousands of dollars per year, and the automation cost less than $50,000.

Unfortunately, I had already made this a big public issue when I found out that the personnel grading system was based in part on how many people you supervised. By cutting the twenty jobs, the division director would have lost an entire pay grade.

I ended up making him mad, causing a big stink, and losing credibility in the process.

Some situations exist in the organization because they are to the personal benefit of one or more people. Changing the situation may be beneficial to the organization as a whole, but really negative for certain parties. That doesn't mean you shouldn't recommend those ideas, but it's important to know about any such situations and take them into account. The best strategy is to find a way to modify your idea so that the organization gets all or most of the benefits without those parties being hurt.

3. *How much credibility do you have?* The quality of the idea itself isn't the only thing considered in evaluation—the quality of the presenter of the idea has a lot to do with whether it's accepted. Your own performance history, your track record on other projects, your current rank and status, and your length of service in the organization are all part of what's considered.

The bigger or more far-reaching the consequences of your idea or proposed change, the more you should expect to have your personal credibility examined. Not only should you make sure you're on top of your other work issues and that your performance is exemplary, you should also consider whether you are the best person to champion your idea. Some ideas will only be considered if they come from a person of a certain rank, or from someone with a particular organizational or professional background. It may be in your best interest to give away the idea or share it with someone with the power to make it happen.

4. *How many ideas do you have out there?* You'll be a lot more credible and accomplish more change if you limit the number of ideas you generate and sell at any one time. Add more ideas as you achieve results from other ideas. If you're the sort of person who just keeps thinking them up, write them down and hold them for later. Prioritize the ideas you come up with, looking for the best ratios of risk/reward/resources. Do some preliminary investigation on new ideas to winnow out those ideas that may not fly so you shoot them down yourself rather than have management shoot them down for you. Consider giving away your ideas to those who can champion them, expanding your influence and results that way.

SELLING YOUR IDEAS

1. Do you understand the situation sufficiently?

    _____

    How can you improve your understanding?

    _____

    _____

2. Whose oxen might be gored?

    _____

    How can you reduce the negative impact?

    _____

    _____

3. How much credibility do you have?

    _____

    How can you build your credibility?

    _____

    _____

4. How many ideas do you have out there?

    _____

    Which ones are worth pursuing?

    _____

    _____

Chapter

Check Your Priorities
With the Big Picture

In many organizations, it seems as if everything is an urgent #1 priority. Sorting out the real "urgent #1's" from the not-so-real "urgent #1's" is a key skill for productivity and personal stress management.

To make sure that your priorities are in sync with the boss's, department's, and organization's priorities, you must first learn what those are, which you have done in previous chapters.

Beware, however, because priorities are slippery, especially when it comes to daily work assignments. The confusion of "urgent" (time pressure) with "important" (value) is the key reason why it's hard to maintain focus. By keeping your focus on the big picture—those things that must be accomplished to ensure the organization's mission is accomplished—you can evaluate your daily priorities on a regular basis to make sure you're going in the right direction.

Knowing your objectives—your mission-critical goals—is the foundation of your ability to make meaningful, legitimate decisions about priorities. That's your priorities, your boss's, your organization's, or anyone else's.

The core question is always and necessarily "why?" Any discussion of the value of a given assignment or project has to come back to the "why." If there's no good answer to the "why," that ought to be a big hint that maybe it's not that important a priority in the first place.

On any project that takes more than a few days, you may want to periodically recheck the priority. One of the most common problems you'll find is that the reason for a job assignment has evaporated but the job assignment continues anyway. A classic and probably apocryphal story has it that an American general attended a military ceremony in Great Britain. Five soldiers fired a cannon salute. One man loaded the cannon, one man aimed the cannon, one man fired the cannon, and one man barked out the commands. The fifth man stood at attention during the ceremony, then marched off with the other four.

"What does the fifth man do?" asked the American general.

His hosts were surprised at the question. "Why, he's the fifth man, of course!" came the reply.

He repeated the question, and finally his hosts became curious and investigated. It turned out that the job of the fifth man, in the days of cavalry, was to hold the horses.

The need had long since evaporated, but the tradition lived on.

Ask, "Why am I doing this?" more often. It's the easiest and best tool you have to keep things straight. And sometimes it's a powerful way to eliminate unnecessary work. As the saying goes, "Never put off until tomorrow what you can put off until the day *after* tomorrow, because you might not have to do it at all the day after tomorrow."

QUICK TIP SELF-ASSESSMENT

1. List your current daily priorities. For each priority, ask: "Why am I doing this right now?"

   _____

   _____

   _____

2. For each priority in which the "why" question doesn't have a good answer, can you delete, delegate, or postpone the assignment?

   _____

   _____

   _____

3.   Is your boss an "urgency addict"? Are you?

     _____

     _____

     _____

Chapter

33

Recognize Your Boss's Humanity

Bosses are people, too. Because of the hierarchical difference, that's a surprisingly easy fact to overlook. Bosses are prone to self-doubt, lack of assertiveness, insecurity, fear, confusion, and paranoia, just like everyone else in the organization. Because of the power dynamic, however, such human weaknesses are amplified in their impact. "When the boss sneezes, everyone catches cold," as the saying goes.

The humanity of your boss may also be hidden because the organizational culture demands it. Bosses are always and necessarily role models for appropriate behavior, and your boss may work very hard to conceal his or her emotional state. When the emotions leak out, they may be so camouflaged that you may mistake them for rational decisions.

You may not be able to officially acknowledge your boss's humanity, but always keep it in mind. Not only will the simple fact of your acceptance modify your behavior in the right direction, you'll find that your own anxiety about your boss's moods and issues will lessen.

It's worthwhile to find out all you can about your boss's background, including such issues as family background, work history, college affiliation, awards and honors, organizational memberships, and geographic origins. If your boss isn't open about such information, you may still be able to find out quite a bit. For senior managers, the public relations staff often has bio sheets available for the press. See if you can get copies.

It's possible that there are some points of personal connection with your boss that will help the relationship: You may come from the same area, have gone to the same school, or be members of the same interest group. If you don't have a direct connection, you may be able to develop an indirect one—perhaps someone you know is from the same area, etc.

Some people see any direct effort to build a personal connection with your boss as ethically questionable brown-nosing behavior. However, you can look at it in a much more constructive way by not only learning about your boss but also learning about others on your team.

In George Bernard Shaw's *Pygmalion*, Eliza Doolittle is arguing with Henry Higgins after the ball about how he's treated her. Higgins tells her his manners are the same as his friend Colonel Pickering's. "That's not true," replies Eliza. "He treats a flower girl as if she was a duchess." "And I," replied Higgins, "treat a duchess as if she were a flower girl."[33] Henry Higgins thinks they are the same behavior, but they are not. If you show a high level of human concern for others in general, the question of whether you're brown nosing by treating a superior well simply doesn't arise.

QUICK TIP SELF-ASSESSMENT

1. How comfortable am I with my boss's human weaknesses and foibles?

---

33. Shaw, George Bernard. "Pygmalion." In Weintraub, Stanley, ed. *The Portable Bernard Shaw*. New York: Viking Portable Library, 1977, p. 417.

2. In what ways do those weaknesses and foibles have an impact on me? What can I do about it?

    _____

    _____

    _____

3. How can I do a better job of validating my boss's humanity?

    _____

    _____

    _____

Chapter

Be Aware of What's Going On, but Don't Get "Political"

The term *office politics* has a strongly negative connotation for most people, but as with *networking* and *mentoring*, practicing office politics the right way is a critical skill for survival and growth. Many of the suggestions and ideas you've been reading can be classified as "political," yet they are all principled, appropriate ways to get things done in the organization. They certainly benefit you, but not at the cost of hurting, manipulating, or taking advantage of anyone else, or harming the organization as a whole.

Office politics is a reality in any organization employing three or more people. Office politics is simply the name we use to describe the informal and sometimes emotionally driven process of working out goals among people. The question is not *whether* you play office politics; it's *how* you play. You want to use positive strategies, while avoiding those negative behaviors often called "political." You still have to understand these negative games and what to do about them in managing up.

Avoid underhanded tactics that, while often practiced, tend to ultimately damage the careers of people who use them, such as discrediting others for your personal advantage, covering up unpleasant truths, hogging the credit, sabotaging others' projects.

Be aware that these behaviors are practiced by many people in the organization, and be prepared to defend yourself. (Always make sure you are familiar with many games and tactics you might find ethically inappropriate to use, because you may need to cope when other people use them.)

Some ways to deal with these tactics include:

- Keep good documentation. A good strategy is to keep a daily work diary, but be careful to write only factual information in it, as opposed to opinions and ventings about unpleasant events.
- Consider confrontation, in private and carefully planned, with the goal of negotiating a peace treaty.
- Above all, maintain a record of high integrity and good performance, and many attacks on you will be discounted and not believed.

Getting Power

Engineers define power as energy that overcomes resistance to do work. You need to accumulate power within the organization to achieve your goals. In fact, the most important goal of managing up is to increase your power.

Accumulating power is not a negative or unethical goal in and of itself, as long as the tactics you use to get power and the uses to which you put power are themselves positive and ethical.

Here are some of the sources of effective organizational power—the power that helps you manage up:[34]

1. *Assertiveness is power.* Your personal assertiveness—your willingness to speak up and ask for what you want—gives you legitimate power.

2. *Accomplishment is power.* Your track record and history of successes increases your power and influence.

3. *Knowledge is power.* When you know what you're talking about, people are more likely to listen to you.

4. *Relationships are power.* Networking and mentoring relationships add extensively to your power and influence.

5. *Initiative is power.* The person who actually goes out and does something, who makes the first move, who takes charge, gains power in the process.

34. Dobson, Michael. *Practical Project Management.* Op. cit., pp. 214–218.

6. *People skills are power.* The ability to "work well and play with others" didn't stop mattering in kindergarten. It's a key element in your ability to get results every day.

7. *Communication is power.* "If you don't ask, you don't get." The art of communication involves the ability to articulate your goals and desires and to put them across in persuasive and positive language. Communication gets results.

8. *Understanding is power.* Work at making sure you understand the big picture—how your work and your position fit into the organizational context. Study the dynamics and interactions among the key players. The more you know about people and how they work, the more powerful and effective you'll be in the organization.

Avoid Seeming "Political"

To avoid seeming "political," it's not enough merely to avoid unethical strategies. Some people give the impression that they are more concerned with who's doing what to whom than they are with what the work is and how to get it done.

While it's critical to be plugged in to the informal information channels to make sure you do understand what's going on, the concern you must have and show is that you are there primarily to get a job done and to achieve results for the organization. When that shows in your actions, the relationship-building and negotiating activities that are part of effective politics are then seen as ways to contribute to the work.

What if you adopted the strategy of simply doing an excellent job and avoiding all political behaviors? Wouldn't your reputation and performance achieve the same results? In the real world, unfortunately, the answer is no, or at least not necessarily. Political behavior includes the relationship-building, networking, and influencing strategies that are necessary to get the work done. Office politics permeates all the organization, and it's a reality of life.

DEVELOPING YOUR POLITICAL POWER
(The Four R's)

Your current political power results from four interlocking elements—the Four R's. Define your current level in each and how you might work to increase it:

ROLE
What power results from my current position in the organization (title, official duties, signature authority, committee memberships)?

_____

_____

_____

How could I expand my role power?

_____

_____

_____

RESPECT
What level of credibility and respect have I earned (major accomplishments, personal integrity, job knowledge, problem solving)?

_____

_____

_____

How could I expand my respect power?

_____

_____

_____

RELATIONSHIPS
What relationships do I have inside and outside the organization that develop and expand my personal power and influence (mentors, networks, committees, professional groups, industry contacts)?

_____

_____

_____

How could I expand my relationship power?

_____

_____

_____

RHETORIC
How good are my communications skills (persuasiveness, negotiation, listening, public speaking, group participation, writing)?

_____

_____

_____

How could I expand my rhetoric power?

_____

_____

_____

Chapter

(35)

Sharpen Your Decision Skills

Your influence and power within the organization isn't ever merely that which resides in your job description. A lot of your power involves your ability to make the right decision in the right way at the right time. Decision-making consultant Harvey Kaye points out that decision making is more than just problem solving. While rational problem-solving strategies are part of decisions, decision making has a crucial emotional component. "Real decisions carry the full weight of our convictions; we make them because they *matter* to us. . . . We are willing to endure the costs they entail exactly because they bring benefits that we need and desire."[35]

Oddly enough, according to physics professor and game theory expert H. W. Lewis, the outcome of a decision is a pretty poor guide to whether the decision was a good one. "If something we couldn't possibly have foreseen happens, it isn't fair to have to take the blame if the surprise is bad, and it isn't honest to take the credit if it is good."[36]

Decision making in organizations often takes place in a multiplayer environment. A number of people with individual concerns and objectives start with limited information and often high inher-

35. Kaye, Harvey. *Decision Power: How to Make Successful Decisions With Confidence.* Englewood Cliffs, N.J.: Prentice Hall, 1992, p. xiii.
36. Lewis, H. W. *Why Flip a Coin? The Art and Science of Good Decisions.* New York: John Wiley & Sons, 1997, p. vii.

ent uncertainty, and need to make the best decision under the circumstances.

The study of complex decision making is called "game theory." Statistics, psychology, and the application of sophisticated logical tools come together to discover that often the best decision is not what one's initial intuition would suggest. In fact, there are powerful tools available to improve your decision making, and it will amply repay the investment of your time to study them.

Because the future is inherently unknowable, no decision-making process is infallible. You know you're moving up in the ranks of management the day you discover that they're not really paying you to make good decisions, but rather to make decisions when all the alternatives before you are risky, stinky, and unpleasant. Make your decisions in the best way possible, on a timely basis, and commit to your decisions, even though they may not always be right. And be flexible enough to change your mind when the facts go against you.

QUICK TIP SELF-ASSESSMENT

1.   How good are my decision-making skills?

   _____

   _____

   _____

2.   How confident and firm am I in making my decisions? Can I improve?

   _____

   _____

   _____

3.   What organizational culture characteristics shape the decision-making process where I work?

   _____

   _____

   _____

Chapter

36

Consider Your Boss
a Customer

Customer service is one of the key management focuses of the current day, because customers are the people who ultimately keep you in business. Companies involved in the quality movement take the customer service concept a bit further by using the idea of the "internal customer," who is anyone inside the organization who uses our work product and who provides a service or a product we need to do our work.

By this definition, your boss should be considered one of your key customers. Use the ideas and philosophies of effective customer service to improve your relationship and your ability to manage up.

How do you treat a customer? First, with respect and concern for his or her needs. Second, with the ingredients of politeness and good manners. Third, with excellent listening skills. Fourth, with the goal of meeting his or her needs and wishes.

In a customer relationship, there is a trade for mutual benefit. If you buy something in a store, you get what you purchased and the store gets your money. If you're satisfied with your purchase and the store has made a profit, everybody wins. If you feel good about your overall shopping experience, you're likely to go back and shop there again.

In an internal customer relationship, there is still value exchanged, even if it's not always cold, hard cash. If we treat our boss as a customer, the boss's needs are met, the departmental objectives are satisfied, and the company does better. Of course, the cash we get in our paycheck is part of our reward for providing that customer service. But the other goals, such as career advancement, more interesting work assignments, and a more pleasant place to work, are advanced as well.

Anything that advances the customer relationship between you and your boss increases your effectiveness in managing up.

QUICK TIP SELF-ASSESSMENT

1. In what ways can I consider my boss my customer?

    _____

    _____

    _____

2. What customer-service techniques could I use to improve my ability to manage up?

    _____

    _____

    _____

Chapter

37

Work on Better Communication

A s nationally known training expert Fred Pryor once observed, "If dogs could talk, we probably wouldn't get along with them, either."

Communications skills are another area to which every professional can devote time and effort. *Assertive* means to open your mouth and say what you mean. If you're overloaded, say so. If you don't understand the assignment, say so. If you don't say what you want, don't expect to have your mind read. *Clear* means to send your messages in a way that is most easily understood. Don't make other people work to decipher your messages.

How to Say "No"

One key element in managing up is knowing the right way to say "no" to a boss or other superior. Clearly, your goal is to have your "no" accepted without negative consequences. One way to achieve this is to separate the task from the person—you want to reject the request or order without rejecting the person who gives it to you. Here's a simple process that separates the person from the problem, and deals with each in turn:

- *Validate.* Start with a statement of understanding and support, for example, "I understand this (whatever the person is talking about) is important." You say those words, but what you really mean is "I understand *you* are important."

- *Postpone*. Offer objective, external support for the idea that you have to decline to get involved right now, for example, "I'm right in the middle of the report you said you wanted by noon."
- *Options*. Offer an alternative that focuses on what you *can* do, for example, "Let's do this. Why don't we meet in the conference room from 2:00 to 2:15 this afternoon?"
- *Choices*. Or, offer a forced choice, for example, "Would you prefer that I start on the new task immediately and finish the report tomorrow, or would you prefer I finish the report by noon and then meet with you this afternoon?"

How to Turn Down a Work Assignment When You're Overloaded

A critical element in managing up is knowing how to turn down a job assignment when you're overloaded. Here are three steps that should always be part of your method:

- *Recognize* your boss' authority to give you the assignment.
- *Provide* facts and data to show your current workload.
- *Offer* a choice, not an ultimatum.

When you're given a new job assignment and you're overloaded, the choice you offer is about the relative priority of the assignment, not "I can't do this," but "How does this fit in with my other priorities?" Instead of saying no to the new assignment, you're simply saying no to the impossible. Something's got to give, but your boss has the power in most cases to decide. You provide information about options if you can, but when you give your boss the opportunity to decide, the potential negativity goes way down.

Will this work for you? You might be thinking, "My boss wouldn't stand for any discussion about priority. He or she would say, 'Just get them all done,' and drop it on my desk." Try some of these:

- *Keep current project lists*. If you simply state you're overloaded or have too many other projects, and can't back it up with proof, you may find that you don't have credibility. Keep a running list of project assignments, along with time estimates and priorities, so that instead of saying, "I'm overloaded," you can show a list of the work and say, "How and where do you want this new work put in with my other priorities?"

- *Say it again, firmly.* Sometimes you'll need to repeat, firmly and assertively, what you just said in order to have it taken seriously. You may have to do it several times. The "broken record" technique is a classic tool of assertiveness training, and it's designed to overcome a certain type of opposition. Kids learn that parents, for example, have a certain number of "no's." If they ask often enough—if they have one more "yes" than their parent has "no's"—they win. Quite a few adults carry the memory of that technique and use it. The "broken record" technique is a way to show you have "no's" to spare.

- *Make a list and have a meeting.* If you don't happen to have a list ready at just the right moment, you can make it later. Prioritize the assignments as best you can, using the information you have. Include the job assignment you've been given. Arrange a meeting with your boss and show him or her the list. "I'd like to make sure I've got the items on my list in the right order of priority for you," you state, and give a copy of the list to your boss.

- *Have the right attitude.* To make this approach work, you must also not fall into an erroneous idea shared by many employees—that it is your boss's job to keep track of your current workload. It isn't your boss's responsibility at all. It's yours. Your boss is not required to realize that you are overloaded if you haven't told him or her. Therefore, you have no reason for anger or resentment, so those emotions don't enter into it.

Polish Your General Communications Skills

Evaluate your communications effectiveness and consider working on some of the following areas:

- *Clarity.* Nothing else matters if your message isn't heard and understood by the recipient. Do you use the right, powerful word in each case? Can you paint word pictures to get your message across?

- *Understanding.* Getting your message accepted by the listener requires that you have some understanding of the listener and his or her own agenda. Remember the world's most popular radio station is **WIIFM**, the "What's in It for Me" network!

- *Correctness.* Proper grammar doesn't only help with clarity, it's essential for your professional image. People judge your social

class, professionalism, education, competence, intelligence, and
credibility by your grammar.

- *Listening.* All good talkers must also be good listeners. Picking up
  nonverbal cues by your observation of your audience helps you
  adjust your message to make sure it is understood and accepted.
- *Nonverbal communication.* Tone of voice and nonverbal communication (body language, dress, and grooming) make up the majority of the message received by others. Are you showing the right
  image as well as saying the right words?

Public speakers frequently videotape or audiotape themselves
so they can see themselves as others see them. Only by getting an
outside perspective on yourself can you truly see how you can
change to become more effective.

Communication in a Hierarchy

Communication in the world of business has an additional problem:
It takes place in a hierarchy, often between people who are not
equals. Understanding how the presence of hierarchy shapes your
communications as well as those of others is important.

Philosopher and satirist Robert Anton Wilson (writing as Hag-
bard Celine) describes "Celine's Second Law": Communication is
only possible between equals.[37] (More formally, "Accurate communication is only possible in a nonpunishing situation.") We began
this book with a discussion of the invisible gun carried by managers.
One consequence, as Wilson observes, is, "[A] man with a gun (the
power to punish) is told only what his target thinks will not cause
him to pull the trigger."

There is an innate tendency to lie—or, more politely, to shade
the truth in favor of the consensus we perceive in management—
that is hard (arguably impossible) to erase in a hierarchical structure. It certainly seems easier to be a yes-man, and some managers
tend to surround themselves with yes-men. But the situation is more
complex.

When you act as if the gun (punishing power) is of great significance, it becomes of real significance. When you ignore the gun
for the most part, behaving as if it's not there and communicating
honestly and clearly, the interesting phenomenon is that the gun
becomes less real—there is less power to punish you. In fact, figur-

---

37. Wilson, Robert Anton. *The Illuminati Papers.* Ronin Publishing: Berkeley, Calif., 1990, pp. 122–125.

ing this out is often one of the steps new employees have to discover in order to be qualified for promotion. Some people cower forever under the perception of a threat; others learn to recognize that the threat is at least partly illusory, and therefore qualify to advance in the game.

We've emphasized the concept of assertiveness several times, and once again we see why personal assertiveness is one of the keys to managing up. Submitting to the power of the hierarchy is a way to lose. The paradox is that fighting back, in a way, acknowledges the reality of the gun every bit as much as submissiveness. Either strategy leads to trouble. As the motto of the movie *War Games* has it, "The only way to win is not to play."

COMMUNICATIONS EFFECTIVENESS ISSUES

1. How successful am I currently at being an assertive communicator?

   _____

   _____

2. What kinds of resistance or problems have I experienced in being assertive about my needs, wants, and goals?

   _____

   _____

3. Do I keep good documentation about my job assignments or projects? What kind of documentation or charting would help my communication?

   _____

   _____

4. What areas of communication could I most effectively develop and work on?

   _____

   _____

Chapter
38

Manage Your Time Effectively

U nless you can manage yourself, you will tend to have little success in managing others, whether down, sideways, or up. The choices you make about your time—how you spend it, how you prioritize it—are at the core of your self-management effectiveness. Since we've learned that your ability to influence others involves getting your own act together first, evaluate your personal time management on a regular basis.

- *Take time to plan.* The common saying, "If you don't have time to do it right, when will you find time to do it over?" should influence your commitment to good planning. Set aside a minimum amount of time each day for planning. Even five or ten minutes a day spent with your personal organizer will make a difference. Prioritize your assignments. Don't be one of the people who manages by a "to-do" list: You end up prioritizing by how many lines you can cross off each day, which tends to push you into focusing on trivia. (If you've ever done something not on your to-do list and wrote it on afterward so you could then cross it off, you may be guilty of this.)
- *Learn to say "no"—and make it stick.* You can't say "yes" to things that don't matter without automatically saying "no" to the productive things you might have done with the same time. Practice the assertive ways of refusing job assignments and time-wasters that you learned in the previous chapter.

- *Put off procrastination.* One technique for overcoming, or at least lessening, the amount of procrastination in your life is to remember that procrastination is always a motivated behavior. You don't procrastinate because you are some strange creature known as a procrastinator. Instead, there's a motive. Look for the underlying cause of the motivation, work to overcome the obstacles, and above all, learn to work in small segments. The hardest part is usually getting started. A little bit—even fifteen minutes—at a time, adds up at a surprising rate.
- *Develop and maintain good work habits.* One element of being a professional is developing and maintaining good work habits. Messy desks, chronic lateness, sloppy notes, excessive socializing, personal calls, long lunches—are you guilty of any of these poor work habits? If so, resolve to make changes.

QUICK TIP SELF-ASSESSMENT

1. How well do I manage my time—am I guilty of any of the poor time-management habits described here?

   _____

   _____

   _____

2. What benefits could I get from improving my time management?

   _____

   _____

   _____

3. What are some specific ways in which I could start improving my personal and professional time management?

   _____

   _____

   _____

Chapter

39

Take Your Job Seriously, but Take Yourself Lightly

The effective and proper use of humor is an important element in your overall communications and managing up strategy. The two most important characteristics of business humor are skill and appropriateness. You don't need to learn to be a stand-up comedian (such people have mastered the skill part, but not always the business appropriateness part), but you do need some basic skills.

If you have a reputation for no sense of humor, or inability to tell a joke, observe those who are good at it. Notice that people with a good sense of office humor are self-deprecating, don't overdo it, and follow three rules: They don't drag out the set-up too long, they don't telegraph the punch line, and they don't laugh while they're telling the joke. Consider memorizing and practicing a joke in private rather than simply winging it.

The appropriate part of office humor is most crucial. Is the joke relevant to the office situation? Does it put people at ease or break the tension? Avoid risky humor, ranging from group stereotypes (unless you're making fun of your own group), to sarcasm, "playful" insults, practical jokes, and "off-color" humor.

One reason that people get in trouble using humor is that humor is often thin camouflage for underlying hostility and aggression. "I was only kidding" and "Can't you take a joke?" are ways people deny what is often their actual intent. Jokes are deadly serious. Psychiatrist Martin Grotjahn is very blunt: "Wit is related to aggression, hostility, and sadism; humor is related to depression, narcisissm, and masochism."[38]

If you can avoid some of the traps in badly chosen humor, there can be real benefits from using humor in the workplace, for yourself and others:

- *Humor lowers stress and promotes teamwork.* One seminar company had a contest among its speakers for their single most embarrassing public-speaking disaster. Not only were the stories themselves funny, but newer speakers gained confidence that if they made a mistake, it was not necessarily going to be fatal.
- *Being able to laugh at yourself makes you stronger.* Laughing at your own weaknesses makes others feel that your shortcomings can't be very serious. It defuses potential criticism and makes you more likeable, more easily followed.
- *Laughing reduces stress and improves health.* Laughing stimulates the release of endorphins, the body's natural painkillers. Endorphins give us a sense of well-being and confidence, and may even strengthen the immune system!

If you tell jokes, appreciate the humor of others as well. A person who is a good audience often has people more willing to appreciate his or her own sense of humor.

QUICK TIP SELF-ASSESSMENT

1. How good is my office sense of humor? Do I know how to laugh at work?

_____

_____

_____

38. Grotjahn, Martin. *Beyond Laughter: Humor and the Subconscious.* New York: McGraw-Hill, 1970, p. 33.

2. What are my weaknesses in telling jokes and generating laughter?

    _____

    _____

    _____

3. What steps can I take to show that I take my job seriously, but take myself lightly?

    _____

    _____

    _____

Chapter

40

Build Your Skills and Knowledge in Management

There are hardly any problems you have or will ever have that haven't been faced or solved by someone else. Management is an exhaustively studied topic, and this book is only one example. Read, listen to tapes, and watch videos to learn more about the art of management. As you develop your skills, you will advance in your career. That's true not only because of the improvements in your skills and abilities, but also because of the interest and enthusiasm you show for professional growth. It's amazing what a small percentage of the workforce actively takes the initiative for personal and professional growth and development; such people advance and are promoted far out of proportion to the degree of their representation.

There are certain collateral skills you need in your career in addition to the core technical and management knowledge you need to do your job.

Management and Supervision

Basic concepts of management and supervision are part of every organization. You must understand these key concepts:

- *Supervisory styles.* Supervisory or management styles are roughly divided into task-centered and people-centered approaches. Task-centered supervision emphasizes clear instructions, defined tasks, and regular procedures. People-centered supervision emphasizes relationships, questioning, learning, and self-development. Neither task-centered nor people-centered is right or wrong. Instead, the choice depends more on the nature of the job.

- *Delegating.* Delegating is the process of getting someone else to carry out some part of your responsibility by giving them instructions, tools, and the necessary authority. The failure to learn to delegate well is the single biggest reason why some managers fail.
- *Motivating.* Have you ever met an unmotivated person? While most people would answer "Yes!" the right answer is "No." Think about it: Have you ever met people who spend more energy scheming to get out of the work than it would take to do it and get it over with? Are they unmotivated? No, they are highly motivated—just in a different direction. Motivation simply describes the reasons why people do the things they do. If you want them to do something different, you must change the payoffs.

It's a good idea to learn about the key thinkers and names in management and supervision. One reason you see so many references in this book is to give you other places to look. Take the time to learn about management thinkers such as Ken Blanchard (*One Minute Manager*), Peter F. Drucker, Warren Bemis, Marvin Weisbord, and Frederick Herzberg. You'll run into their names often.

Finance and Accounting

Finance is the language of senior management. Even if your job isn't primarily oriented toward finance, it's essential to understand it. Wharton professor Dr. Steven Finkler observes, "The non-financial manager can no longer avoid financial information. Profit statements, operating budgets, and project analyses are a constant part of the manager's day. Once you understand a few basics you can fight back and demand information [from accountants] that is both useful and usefully explained."[39]

Basic accounting concepts such as assets and liabilities, debits and credits, are part of the normal dialogue within the organization. Learn what the key financial statements are: balance sheet, income statement, sources and uses of cash statement. Learn how to read them. The organization's financial condition may be stated in terms

39. Finkler, Steven A. *The Complete Guide to Finance & Accounting for Non-financial Managers.* Englewood Cliffs, N.J.: Prentice Hall, 1983, p. xiii.

of financial ratios, such as return on investment, return on assets, and return on equity. These terms aren't synonyms. Depreciation and inventory costing can turn the financial picture of the organization completely upside down.

Once you've got a basic handle on these concepts, start reading the business section of the paper regularly and consider subscribing to one or more of the standard business magazines or newspapers. You'll get the executive perspective about what's going on, which will always translate into greater power, reach, and influence on your part.

Project Management

Project management is also part of every job, sooner or later. While you may not need to understand the intricacies of calculating uncertainty on the critical path, you need at least the basics of Gantt charting and project organization. Above all, you need to know how to think like a project manager to meet your challenges and achieve your goals.

Steps in project management. All projects begin by determining their objective:

- First, ask "Why?"
- Second, use this information to determine the "Triple Constraints": budget, time, and performance criteria.
- Third, break the project into tasks—the larger the project, the greater detail in the breakdown.
- Fourth, put the tasks in a project sequence, the order in which the tasks will be performed. A Gantt Chart is a timeline that shows how long the tasks will take and how the tasks fall in a sequence. For example, if Task A takes a week at the start of the project, and Task B takes two weeks but can start only when Task A is complete, the Gantt Chart looks like this:

| Task | Week 1 | Week 2 | Week 3 |

- Fifth, use the Gantt Chart to track your project by comparing how long each task took to plan.

Managing multiple projects. Normally, the study of project management focuses on managing a single project. The most common situation you will likely find, however, is that you must manage multiple projects simultaneously. If you manage multiple projects, you're no stranger to stress. Frequently, multiple-project managers end up working extra hours, feeling overloaded, and sometimes failing to achieve their goals.

Here are some key elements about managing multiple projects, called "project portfolios":[40]

Task-oriented projects are relatively small in amount of work and time. Each project might take only a few hours, or at most a day or two, if you could handle them in an uninterrupted fashion. But that's not the case. Task-oriented projects are difficult, both because they are often numerous and because the person responsible normally has a full-time regular job to do.

Independent project portfolios consist of projects that are not directly connected to one another. If one should fail (or succeed beyond expectations), it doesn't greatly affect the other projects in the portfolio. The challenge in managing independent project portfolios is that you normally have a fixed amount of resources (people, tools, equipment, and money) available to get them all done. Planning and allocating those resources becomes easier when you use the right techniques.

Interdependent project portfolios are large projects in themselves. However, many of the tasks in the large project are so complex and time-consuming that they are essentially projects in their own right. With an independent portfolio, we know the projects are not connected to each other. However, in an interdependent portfolio, they are very connected. The success of the overall portfolio depends on all of the projects in it being accomplished successfully. The interdependent project portfolio includes all the issues of an independent portfolio and some special issues of its own.

Remember the value of knowledge in developing your power and influence. Study not just what you need to get today's job done, but also what will get you where you want to be tomorrow.

40. Dobson, Michael. *The Juggler's Guide to Managing Multiple Projects.* Sylva, N.C.: Project Management Institute, 1999, p. 5.

MANAGEMENT STUDIES

1. Develop a personal knowledge chart with areas for growth

Topic	Current Knowledge	Needs for Advancement	Additional Resources
Management/ Supervision			
Finance/ Accounting			
Project Management			
Technical Job Skills			
Skills for Next Position			

2. What organizational resources (training programs, company-paid courses, tape/video libraries, etc.) exist to develop my skills?

   _____

   _____

   _____

3. What are the next steps I can take on my own?

   _____

   _____

   _____

Chapter

41

Develop Your Writing Skills

A recent survey revealed that lack of crucial communication skills accounts for 80 percent of why people don't get promoted. Many people actually turn down job promotions because they are afraid their writing and speaking skills won't measure up to those required in higher-level positions.[41]

It's surprising to realize that you can quickly and easily improve your writing skills if you remember the essential rule for writing as effective communication: Write in your own voice. You do this by writing, to the extent possible, the way you talk, and you'll discover that your writing voice becomes more lively, powerful, and engaging. (Of course, for some people that means you should work on your speaking ability.) People regularly speak in simple, clear, easy-to-understand sentences, and when you write in the same way, your writing becomes much easier to understand and accept. Your grammar becomes better, too. It's much more difficult to get it wrong in a short sentence; it's nearly impossible not to get it wrong in a very long one.

The poet Alexander Pope observed, "True ease in writing comes from art, not chance / As those move easiest who have learn'd to dance."[42] Don't shy away from the opportunity to write:

41. Pachter, Barbara, and Marjorie Brody. *Climbing the Corporate Ladder: What You Need to Know and Do to Be a Promotable Person.* Mission, Kans.: SkillPath Publications, 1995, p. 63.
42. Pope, Alexander. *An Essay on Criticism*, lines 362–363, in Tillotson,

The more you do it, the easier it will get. One practical tip is to listen to yourself speak what you are planning to write, then just write it down—that's the easiest way to get a good conversational tone.

Sample file. Another quick tip on improving your writing comes from the old saying, "Amateurs borrow—professionals steal." While the sin of plagiarism is still considered one of the worst things a writer can do, there are a number of ways to borrow that are legitimate and appropriate.

For example, there are numerous books of standard business letters that provide a paragraph-by-paragraph outline. You can also get them on disk for your computer, making editing even quicker and easier. Remember, no one expects a business letter to be a model of unique writing. The reader wants to extract quick information and get back to work.

Keep a file of the best letters you receive or see to build your own database. You can do the same for reports, memos, and the other documents you must write each day.

QUICK TIP SELF-ASSESSMENT

1. How good are my writing skills right now? How do I feel about the act and process of writing?

   _____

   _____

2. What feedback do I get about my writing from my boss and others?

   _____

   _____

3. What are some resources I might use to improve my writing skills?

   _____

   _____

Geoffrey, Paul Fussell, Jr., and Marshall Waingrow. *Eighteenth Century Literature.* New York: Harcourt, Brace & World, 1969, pp. 554–564.

Chapter

Learn How to Train Others

With more than $200 billion a year spent on formal and informal employee education and training, it's vital for all levels of management in the organization—not just human resource professionals and trainers—to understand how to make training work in building productive teams.

Organizations today need a commitment to training as a critical element in their success. Training involves changing or improving the skills of others, and it can be done informally through such processes as on-the-job training, or formally through training seminars and classroom instruction. At least some basic training skills need to be part of what you have to offer in successfully managing up.

You need to understand how training works, how to use training effectively, how to design training, and how to deliver it. Most of all, you need to know how to make training work within the organization—even when you don't always have the support and understanding you need from other managers, supervisors, and even executives.

Training effects change in three distinct areas:

- *Skills.* Technical training, management skills training, and communications training aim at changing the skill level of specific team members.
- *Knowledge.* Training that provides information, background, and insight aims to equip people with the knowledge to make better decisions.

- *Attitudes.* Attitude training provides skills and information to help change attitudes, feelings, and beliefs about the organization and the work.

Training doesn't solve all problems. You may have had the experience yourself of going to a training seminar and coming back excited about new ideas or new information, only to find that your supervisor insists that it be done "the way we've always done it." Or, you may come back excited, only to realize that the culture and even the formal structures and systems of your organization will continue to reward the old ways of doing things.

For training to be effective, it must not stand completely on its own. Management plays a critical role in deciding—by its behavior and its attitudes—whether the training will achieve change or not. The appropriate follow-up and/or the necessary changes in structure, process, procedures, and policies must happen, or training will not be as effective as it could be.

All training is ultimately about improving productivity, and improved productivity makes the organization more competitive, more effective, more profitable, and more successful. Take any opportunity to learn about training, such as "Train the Trainer" seminars and public speaking, that involves training techniques.

QUICK TIP SELF-ASSESSMENT

1. How able am I to train others to do the things I need them to do?

    _____

    _____

2. In what ways does my boss need training and development in core skill areas?

    _____

    _____

3. What resources can I use to become a better trainer?

    _____

    _____

Chapter

43

Arrange for Your Own Performance Appraisals on a Regular Basis

Does your organization have annual, formal performance appraisals? Although it's a strongly recommended practice, many companies don't bother. Even when there is a system in place, a number of supervisors do performance appraisals poorly, thoughtlessly, and at the last minute. That's too bad, because performance appraisals, properly used, can be an effective tool for managing up as well as down.

The only way for performance appraisal to be meaningful is to start with clear, concise, and realistic performance objectives. The value of such objectives for management is clear: They help focus employee performance on critical issues.

The unrecognized limit in this process is that many supervisors and managers haven't completely thought through what those critical job elements happen to be, and as a result both fail to focus on them in the first place and find themselves changing their minds—and their departmental emphasis—day by day or even hour by hour! One of the core concepts of Total Quality Management is that the best quality improvements often come from the bottom up, since the best specific suggestions for improvement usually come from the people closest to the problem. As a general rule, you know the details of your work better than your boss. That's an opportunity for you.

We can easily see why good performance objectives help managers. What needs to be equally clear is how they can benefit you as an employee and team member. First, performance objectives can—and should—be negotiated. Remember that your boss has many things on her or his mind, and your performance objectives are only one of them—and not necessarily the most important one. This gives you an opportunity to participate in setting your own goals and objectives, and you can use those to your career advantage while still being fully supportive of your organization. Let's look at some ideas you can use:

- *Identify (and negotiate) critical job elements.* The supervisor must identify critical job elements, and your understanding of them is crucial to their identification. Think through the critical elements of your job as you understand it, write down those elements, and have them ready when negotiating next year's performance objectives.
- *Identify potential conflicts between your vision and your boss's vision.* What if you find there is a conflict between your boss's vision and your own? In the real world, your boss's vision ultimately trumps your own if you're unable to negotiate a mutually agreeable solution. If this is the problem, check some of the earlier sections of this book to deal with vision conflicts.
- *Identify your own developmental goals.* Think about your improvement goals both in terms of the position you hold and in terms of your long-term career goals, and be prepared to discuss them. It's difficult for many managers to discuss frankly the problems they may have with team members and employees. By turning the topic from potential criticism toward improvement, you make it easier for a manager to provide you with necessary feedback. In addition, developmental goals aren't necessarily about your faults. Instead, they can be about your opportunities for growth.
- *Identify the job assignments and goals necessary for promotability and advancement.* Obviously, you need to focus on and accomplish the goals that are central to the position you now hold. In addition, however, you need to identify the types of job assignments, projects, and tasks necessary to achieve the next rung on the management ladder (or another career target you have) and try to incorporate achieving those into your performance and develop-

mental objectives for the next rating period. When they're part of
your performance standards, it's easier to get the time, priority,
and resources to accomplish them. Don't forget committees, task
forces, interdepartmental groups, and other assignments that
expand your contacts and networks within (and outside) the
organization.
- *Establish SMART criteria.* The acronym "SMART" stands for "Specific, Measurable, Agreed upon, Realistic, and Timely," and de-
fines the necessary qualities for a good goal or objective. One easy
way to get yourself into trouble in developmental goals or objectives is to settle for vague or ill-defined ones. If you can't define
when or whether you reach them, your appraisal is a matter of
management whim, not facts.
- *Write a training plan for yourself.* Part of a developmental plan
should be training goals. What courses, workshops, or degree programs would improve your ability to perform your current job
and help fit you for the next level? What are your current organization's policies on training? There's often a training budget that
is separate from your department's budget. If so, find the criteria
for using it and take advantage of training opportunities to the
maximum.
- *Provide regular feedback to your boss.* In the real world, a twelve-
month performance appraisal tends to be about whatever you did
(or failed to do) in the last two or three months, because memories
tend to be short term rather than long term. Management books
everywhere focus on your need for feedback from your managers;
your managers need feedback from you as well. Provide regular
updates on what you've been doing, the progress you've made
toward your defined goals, and obstacles that may prevent you
from meeting them fully. See the next managing up tip for more
details on how to do this.

What If Your Appraisal Goes Against You?

What if you get a bad performance appraisal, or one you think
doesn't do you justice? There are ways to limit the damage.
  There are actions you should definitely avoid:

- *Don't refuse to sign the appraisal.* In most organizations, your signature on the appraisal only means that you've read it and had the
opportunity to discuss it, not that you agree with it. Refusal to
sign only shows that you don't understand the situation, which

will make you look worse in the eyes of any level of management that reviews the appraisal.

- *Try to recognize any truths in the appraisal, even if they're buried.* Even if the overall appraisal gives a wrong or misleading impression about your performance, there well may be some truths in it. If you end up protesting or challenging the appraisal, your failure to recognize any legitimate criticisms will count against you in the eyes of reviewing managers.

- *Avoid the temptation to write a scathing rebuke.* Or, if you can't resist the temptation, write the scathing rebuke at home to calm yourself down, and then write your comments when you're more settled. Your only real defense against a bad appraisal is by means of facts. If it's simply your opinion of your performance against your boss's, rank wins. Any written appeal or protest needs to identify a factual basis for giving you a better rating than the one you got.

- *Decide how much it really matters.* In some organizations, a lot is at stake in performance appraisals, from your next raise or bonus to your real eligibility for promotion. In other organizations, appraisals have little effect. Make sure your response to a poor or unfair appraisal is proportional to the amount of damage it can do to you. (And if it is patently unfair, prejudicial, and does you great harm, you might consider paying a private visit to an attorney who specializes in these matters.)

- *Negotiate.* If you approach it correctly, you may discover that an appraisal can be negotiated. If the organization has time-consuming grievance or appeal mechanisms, it may be better for both parties to reach a fair compromise on their own. Again, focus on specific facts—things you did, problems you solved, work you accomplished—that could alter the basis for your rating. This is especially useful if your rating deficiency is the result of a single (albeit major) botched or failed assignment. Give your boss a face-saving reason that justifies moving your rating up a notch.

- *Focus on solutions, not on problems.* Another powerful response to a poor appraisal is to turn it into a set of SMART criteria for the next rating period. A single poor performance appraisal may not be fatal to your career as long as it's followed by a set of steadily improving ones. Ask for (or recommend) specific criteria for the next appraisal period that will result in a better appraisal. You might also ask for an interim appraisal, say in three months or so, to benchmark and confirm the desired improvement.

What If Your Organization Doesn't Appraise Performance?

Many organizations, especially smaller ones, don't have a formal appraisal system, or have one on paper but don't actually get around to it. There are enough advantages to you as an employee in having your performance appraised and in negotiating standards that you might want to negotiate your own performance appraisals on a regular basis even if the organization as a whole doesn't do them. Here's how to proceed:

- *Keep it informal.* Names matter. Calling your request for objective setting and feedback a "performance appraisal" may put unnecessary and unproductive pressure on your boss. Keep the request in casual and informal language, specifying precisely what you want without getting into terms that may be loaded in ways you don't like. "Boss, I'd like to find a way to get more regular and specific feedback on what I've been doing. I think I can do more work that meets your needs if we can set together some specific goals for what my highest priorities ought to be. Could we sit down next Tuesday and talk about it?"
- *Do the work yourself.* The more you prepare what you want, the better your chance of getting it. Identify the performance objectives you want, the developmental goals you have set, the issues on which you want feedback. Write them down in a clear list. If you make your boss do all the work, you'll be less likely to get it in the first place, and will end up with a product less tailored to your needs in the second.
- *Identify benefits to your boss.* Help your boss see the clear payoffs in giving you what you want—clearer and mutually established goals for performance, a personal commitment to accomplishment. Lowering the work requirement and increasing the payoff is a proven strategy that gets results with almost any supervisor!

PREPARING FOR PERFORMANCE APPRAISAL

GETTING ORGANIZED

1. What are my organization's current policies and procedures for performance appraisals?

    _____

    _____

    _____

2. In what ways does the practice deviate from the theory?

_____

_____

_____

3. Where am I right now in the performance appraisal cycle?

GETTING RESULTS

1. What are the critical job elements of my position, (a) from my boss's perspective and (b) from my perspective?

_____

_____

_____

2. What conflicts potentially exist between how I see the goals of my job and the way my boss (and the wider organization) see it? If there is a conflict, how should I adjust my vision and how do I want my boss/the organization to adjust its vision?

_____

_____

_____

3. What developmental goals/areas for improvement do I see in myself? Which ones apply primarily to my current job and which to my career goals? What steps could I consider taking to meet these challenges?

_____

_____

_____

4. What specific job assignments and projects would be best for
    me to seek out? What is there about me that would help my
    boss put me forward for those assignments? How else could
    I earn them?

    _____

    _____

    _____

5. What training opportunities would benefit me and the organi-
    zation the most? What is the organization's policy on train-
    ing, and how can I take advantage of it?

    _____

    _____

    _____

6. What specific goals should I identify for the next six months
    or year? How will I keep myself and my boss informed on
    progress and problems?

    _____

    _____

    _____

Chapter

44

Write a "5-15 Report" Each Week

Creativity and new product development consultant Bob Bapes recommends to all his clients that they prepare a "5-15 Report" for their supervisors each week. The title of the report signifies that it should take you no more than fifteen minutes to write and your boss no more than five minutes to read. Bapes says, "I tell [my audience] that if they do this report every week for the next three years, they will double their income and be promoted twice."

The "5-15 Report" is based on the assumption that your boss generally thinks you are good, busy, and productive, but normally only knows 20 to 30 percent of what it is you actually do in your job. Although this concept surprises many people in organizations, it's really a pretty common situation.

Working on the theory that you can't very well be praised or promoted for work your boss doesn't actually know you do, you need to provide a concise, accurate list of your accomplishments on a regular basis.

The "5-15 Report" should be no more than about half a page, and is prepared at the end of each week. The report consists of bulleted information that identifies what you've actually done this week that fits into the following four categories (but don't use these titles specifically):

- How I made the company money this week
- How I saved the company money this week
- Crises I prevented this week
- Where I can use my boss's help in getting something done

By using this system, at the end of your annual performance review period, you'll have fifty pieces of paper in the hands of your boss documenting the meaningful accomplishments for each week for the year. In all likelihood, the records of your competitors are likely to be nonexistent. This will result in more raises, bonuses, and promotions for you—because your boss will know specifically what you're doing for the company.

Bob Bapes identifies the two big fears people have in using this system. The first is the fear that we will not be able to point to weekly accomplishments in these areas. If that's the case, then take a good look at what you're doing so you can refocus your energies on areas that make a difference to the organization. That's a way to improve job security and value.

The second fear is the fear of self-promotion. A reasonable and appropriate amount of self-promotion is critical to your career success, and if this is a problem for you, you need to work on ways of increasing your sense of personal and professional comfort with the idea. Your boss won't know—indeed, can't know—how valuable you are unless you tell him or her on a regular basis.

QUICK TIP SELF-ASSESSMENT

Organize your first "5-15 Report" by making notes on these four critical elements:

How I made the company money this week

_____

_____

_____

How I saved the company money this week

_____

_____

Crises I prevented this week

_____

_____

_____

Where I can use my boss's help in getting something done

_____

_____

_____

Chapter

45

Do More

Best-selling motivational and business author Harvey McKay, upon landing his first sales job, told his father that he intended to make double the income of the other reps. His father replied, "If you want to make twice as much money, you have to make twice as many sales calls."[43]

Why you must do more. This book began with a critical tip that underlies virtually all the other ideas: Do good work. But once you've achieved a certain measure of advancement, good work is no longer a distinguishing characteristic, it is simply assumed. Others who have climbed the initial rungs of the ladder also do good work. You must do more.

Ways to Do More

Spend more time. The first step in doing more is working the extra hours. Great achievers from Fred Astaire to Michael Jordan are known for putting in hour after hour of rehearsal and self-development. While it's important to maintain a goal of a balanced life, remembering the old saying "Nobody on their deathbed ever said, 'Gee, I wish I'd spent more time at the office,' " career-oriented professionals know that 40 hours is the minimum commitment.

43. Dauten, Dale. "Corporate Curmudgeon: Time Expansion—A Window to Creativity," *Chicago Tribune*, 21 February 1999, Section 5, p. 8.

Motivational speaker Zig Ziglar advises that you not stay late, but rather come in early.[44] His rationale is that staying late gives the impression that you can't organize yourself well enough to get your work done on time, but coming in early gives the impression that you can't wait to get a jump start on the day. Remember that appearances count: Take a look at what other peak performers are doing in your organization, and make sure you not only do more, but look like you're doing more.

Accomplish more work. Of course, it's not the number of hours you put in, it's what you get accomplished. In fact, it's increasingly well-established that workaholics—the ones who just can't bring themselves to go home—actually are less productive than those whose schedules are more reasonable.

There are two steps involved in getting more work done in each day. The first step is to move time from the column of unproductive activities into the column of productive activities. The second step is to set clear priorities for the things you can do that will result in real benefits and real accomplishments.

Do work for "extra credit." The best students in high school and college take advantage of opportunities to earn extra credit. Extra-credit projects are available in the workplace too. Look around. Does your department experience repetitive crises that result from the same underlying systems problem that no one ever seems to have time to attack? If so, one of the most valuable extra-credit projects you could possible shoulder would be to attack that problem, thereby eliminating an entire range of crises from the landscape.

Grow your skills. Acquiring and developing new and improved skills also adds to your productivity and allows you to do more. What areas of skill, knowledge, and ability should you target? What resources are available within and outside your organization to help you acquire them? Remember that in most organizations, the primary mode of training and skill development has always been on-the-job training. What tasks and projects can you take on that will improve your abilities in the long run? The best way to learn is often by doing.

44. Ziglar, Zig. *Goals*. Audiotape. Chicago: Nightingale-Conant, 1988.

QUICK TIP SELF-ASSESSMENT

1. How many hours per week do I work now? How do the hours I
    put in compare with those of my colleagues? How can I in-
    crease the hours I put into my job, while still meeting my
    commitments to the rest of my life?

    _____

    _____

    _____

2. Within the hours per week I am at my job, how many of those
    hours am I productive? What unproductive activities occupy
    my day? How can I reduce the time spent in unproductive
    activities?

    _____

    _____

    _____

3. What are the key extra-credit activities, tasks, and projects
    I can seek out that will result in clear benefits for my organi-
    zation? What are the first steps I can take toward achieving
    them?

    _____

    _____

    _____

4. What areas of skill and ability development can I pursue right
    now? What resources are available within my organization?
    What can I do on my own? What can I learn on the job?

    _____

    _____

    _____

Chapter 46

Find the Hidden Keys to the Executive Suite

The executive vice president of a major hotel chain developed a management training program for his staff in the 1970s. "I designed it as a check-off system," he told one of the authors of this book. "For example, if you wanted to become assistant night manager of a Class B property, you could look in a booklet to find the criteria: so many months at the front desk, so many months in the banquet department, this training course and that training course. When you finished the assignments, you filled out a form with the proper information and sent it to the district personnel office to get on the list. When you got to the top of the list, the next available job was yours."

He paused and smiled. "Let me tell you the best part," he said. "I carefully designed it without a rotation plan or other mechanism to allow people to get the assignments and training necessary for promotion."

When he received a blank stare in return, he smiled again. "I want you to remember, in life there are tests and there are tests. The extra test in this system was that if you weren't the type of person who'd stand on your boss's desk and demand the assignments and training you needed, then you weren't the kind of person I wanted running my hotels!"

Types of Hidden Tests

Most organizations aren't as formal and systematic as this, but just about every organization has its own special version of the "hidden keys to the executive suite," the secret tests that, if failed, exclude people from further consideration for promotion. Some are tests of initiative, as in the hotel example, but there are other kinds of tests as well. It's critical to know what the hidden tests are so that you can meet them, beat them, adjust, or look elsewhere.

Initiative tests. Initiative tests, such as our hotel example, are very common. Another supervisor once told one of the authors, "If I don't have to call you down for exceeding your authority from time to time, that tells me you're not ready for any more."

There's nothing inherently unreasonable about requiring proof of initiative in a candidate for promotion or advancement; after all, initiative is a valuable quality. Plus, it's hard to let someone in on the idea that she or he is being tested for initiative without spoiling the test itself.

When confronted with management's seeming indifference as to whether you receive developmental assignments or training, it's a good idea to show initiative and work to get those assignments, whether it's a test of your initiative or not. When a job needs doing, stepping in and doing it is often a good idea, whether or not someone is watching to see who has initiative. With many of the virtues that can be tested secretly, acting on them regardless is often the way to go.

Another general rule to remember is that people tend to promote themselves by taking on extra responsibility, demonstrating initiative and leadership ability, and achieving results. Job titles and money tend to come after the fact to the people who've already proven themselves.

Credential or background tests. Some tests require that you possess certain credentials or backgrounds. Perhaps almost everyone above a certain rank in the organization has an MBA or an engineering degree, whether the job actually requires those qualifications or not. Perhaps the majority of executives went to Ivy League schools, or didn't go to them—one manufacturing executive was overheard to exclaim, "We don't like to hire college-educated people; they never work out."

These kinds of tests are frequently not spoken of aloud, as they can often have the effect (whether consciously or not) of excluding minorities or women from executive ranks. To ferret these tests out, start looking at the qualifications and background of executives and senior managers, looking for patterns that describe the majority of them.

As you identify these tests, look at a couple of factors. First, can you pass the tests, either based on your current qualifications or by acquiring the others? If you can't pass the tests, then take a close look at the executives and senior managers who don't have the usual credentials or backgrounds—and there are almost always at least some of them. How did they get into the senior ranks? Remember that although the tests are real, they are normally not universal. There are secondary ladders you can take.

What are some of the secondary ladders?

First, you can succeed in spite of a lack of certain traditional criteria if you're a lot more competent than everyone else. This has historically been the way minorities and people of lower social classes have gotten their initial footholds. After the first few get in, they hold out a helping hand to others. Therefore, if you find a person who's made it who has a background similar to your own, solicit that person's advice and help.

Second, certain departments (primarily staff departments) are not as sensitive to these special credentials as others. You may find some ladders easier to climb. When you've moved up, you can look for opportunities to move laterally to pick up additional qualifications.

Third, you may discover in your analysis of management backgrounds and patterns that there are two or more parallel sets of these criteria. You can mix and match to develop your own set.

Style and social class tests. The English are famous for "the old school tie," in which the pattern on one's tie identifies the public school one attended. A number of organizations effectively insist that their senior-level staff look like they are members of the upper middle class.

Fortunately, that's relatively easy in the United States, where most class identification signs can be put on or taken off at will. Such factors as "dressing for success" have been exhaustively covered in any number of books. But class covers more than that.

America as a "classless society" is more an ideal than a reality. While class mobility is comparatively easy, it first requires that you understand the game. As essayist Paul Fussell observes, "At the bottom, people tend to believe that class is defined by the amount of

money you have. In the middle, people grant that money has something to do with it, but think education and the kind of work you
do almost equally important. Nearer the top, people perceive that
taste, values, ideas, style and behavior are indispensable criteria of
class, regardless of money or occupation or education."[45]

If this gives you a problem, you're not alone. In a discussion on
this topic, one angry seminar attendee spoke up: "A $500 suit never
did a day's work in its life!" That's true, of course. On the other
hand, a person wearing that $500 suit may well have gotten the ini-
tial opportunity over someone who either refused to wear one or,
worse yet, didn't understand that wearing one would have been
advantageous.

Common interests. You're already familiar with the idea that golf
playing in at least some organizations is a critical executive skill.
First, there's a social class tie-in, the idea that a country club membership establishes you clearly as a member of the upper middle
class. Second, relationship-building and personal marketing efforts
are a legitimate executive skill. Being able to play a game that is
slow paced enough to allow relationship building and networking
(direct job-related discussions are often frowned upon) can be
useful.

The use of clubs, sports, and other special interests is a traditional way for the "old boy network" to exclude others. If exclusive
clubs were simply about some people who wanted to play golf or
tennis together or have a drink with their friends, few would care.
But they're not—or at least they're not about that alone. They're
about who gets to be part of the informal networking that shapes a
significant amount of access to the higher socioeconomic reaches of
American life.

Common interests as a hidden criteria for picking some and
excluding others from the inner management circle can be discriminatory, either deliberately or accidentally. Regardless of the way it
is in your organization, it's important for you to understand how it
works, because understanding is the first key to being able to do
something about it.

How to Uncover Hidden Tests

Hidden tests can be uncovered in different ways. In the case of the
hotel initiative test that began this chapter, one way to pass the test

45. Fussell, Paul. *Class.* New York: Ballantine Books, 1983, p. 3.

is to be naturally the kind of person who behaves in the desired manner. Whether or not you recognize that there has been a test, you pass.

The disadvantage of this approach is that you may not naturally be that type of person, or you may be suppressing your natural tendencies because you're working on the assumption that those behaviors are inappropriate. Fortunately, there are other ways to recognize and potentially pass these hidden tests.

Observation. The first powerful technique is, of course, observation. You should always study the environment you're in. Failure to understand the unofficial environment within your department and within the organization as a whole is almost invariably a disqualification for advancement.

How do you do a good job of observation? One technique is to look for common patterns. Are there specific elements or qualities that the majority of senior managers have in common? Think about our hidden-test concept and reason backward: Is there some behavior or action or style or approach that's common among senior managers? If you can find one, you might be developing a hidden-test clue. "Rounding up the usual suspects"—looking for evidence that some of the specific tests we've described are used in your organization—is often successful as a technique.

A second technique is to look at the people in your organization who have been most successful and who have advanced into senior positions. What personality characteristics, behaviors, or other patterns do most of them have in common? Particularly, has someone succeeded in spite of failures, personality problems, or lack of competence in some key areas? Instead of focusing on why that person should never have been promoted, focus on why that person *was* promoted. Everybody is promoted for a reason—competence, people skills, specific relationships, special project success, or some other factor. It won't always be a reason you agree with or like, but there will always be a reason. Reasons people are promoted in spite of themselves are a good tip-off to hidden tests.

Mentoring. Numerous books and articles talk about the critical necessity of seeking out mentors for your career, and this book recommends developing a network of mentors as well. One of the most valuable services a mentor can provide is tipping you off to the hidden tests that ultimately determine whether you're a promotable person.

For example, if you want to be promoted in the hotel chain, you might simply be the kind of person who shows the initiative necessary to fight for the assignments and training you need. Imagine instead that you develop good mentoring relationships throughout the organization. Sooner or later, someone will take you aside, sit you down, and explain the organizational facts of life. "The point of the promotion system is that you have to push for the training and assignments, not wait for them to come to you."

"Aha!" you say, and now you can rush right out and get to work.

The game is not equal. Some people know the rules in advance; others work in ignorance of the rules. People with good mentor relationships and good network contacts start with better information, which leads necessarily to better results.

FINDING THE HIDDEN KEYS TO ADVANCEMENT

1. What are the official and traditional criteria used in this organization to determine promotability?

   _____

   _____

   _____

2. Who has been promoted and has power in spite of not possessing certain of these characteristics?

   _____

   _____

   _____

3. What behaviors, relationships, attitudes, or interests do these people have in common with others who have also advanced?

   _____

   _____

   _____

4. Who do I know who has the knowledge and insight to identify the hidden keys to advancement who also might be willing to share them with me?

   _____

   _____

   _____

5. What are the likely hidden keys? How can they be demonstrated in practice?

   _____

   _____

   _____

6. What steps and behaviors can I demonstrate to show I possess the hidden keys?

   _____

   _____

   _____

Chapter

Learn the Symbolic Language of the Organization

So, you think you're finally finished with high school? Think again. Many of the same social games, clique identification marks, and status orientations that typified most people's high school experience are alive and well in the organization. It's not necessary to like it; it is necessary to recognize its reality and its seriousness in affecting your relationship with your managers, your promotability, or your power and influence within the organization.

Don't forget it: There's a symbolic language inside your organization that's at least as important—and sometimes more important—than the official language of words and documents that's supposed to run the organization.

Failure to understand the vocabulary of the specific language—the sometimes very specific status symbols and cues that identify the class levels inside the organization—can brand you as someone forever unsuitable for promotion or advancement, someone who doesn't know the rules, or worse, chooses to mock them. That's not to say you can't mock them, or can't choose not to fit in. But you want to make that choice consciously, rather than by accident.

As you identify status symbols and status codes in an organization, you want to use them for your own benefit, to identify yourself as a member of the club, someone who understands how to fit in.

But be careful. The trapping is not the real thing. Author and publishing executive Michael Korda tells this cautionary tale:[46]

> [In one organization, we] found that among the executives status was exactly defined by the kind of thermos that was on their desk. At the lowest levels, the executives had a dark brown or black plastic thermos with one glass.
>
> Higher up they had a chrome plated thermos with two glasses. And at the very top, they had a gold-plated thermos with two glasses and a small gold-plated tray.
>
> What's more, you couldn't fake it. The thermos rule was apparently independent of any other scheme of promotional reward in that corporation, because if you just went out and bought yourself a gold-plated thermos, that would indicate first of all that you didn't understand the rules of the corporation or of the game and that you were therefore unsuitable for further promotion, and probably were making fun of everybody else. Symbols of power matter to people and they matter a lot.

The office caste system helps identify power and status. At Allstate Insurance Company, a fifty-page volume titled "Office Workspace Standards" lists exact office specifications for each level of management. The U.S. Code of Federal Regulations, Subpart 101-17.3, spells out details for Federal offices. Not just size of office, but size and material of desk and chair, windows—they all count when it comes to measuring caste and status.

When one government agency moved into a new building, it acquired new furniture. The building manager found a very nice wooden desk that was being sent to surplus, and decided he wanted it for himself. But the desk had belonged to an assistant director and, in the end, the building manager was forced to give away that desk and buy a new one of appropriate status. Before you condemn this as wasteful, make sure you understand the symbolic vocabulary. It's part of every organization.

46. Korda, Michael. "Power: How to Get It, How to Use It." *What the Pros Say About Success.* Audiotape. New York: American Management Association/Simon & Schuster Audio Division, 1986.

Quick Tip Self-Assessment

1. Identify the status symbols in your organization that identify those with power (corner office, furniture, windows, doors, etc.).

   _____

   _____

   _____

2. What are the more subtle clues that form key distinctions among levels of management (management retreats, certain lunch tables, etc.)?

   _____

   _____

   _____

3. Which of these icons of power are legitimate for me to acquire, and which ones can I get only after I achieve a certain level, rank, or position?

   _____

   _____

   _____

Chapter

Watch the Game Film

Humorist and retail consultant Bob Kramer shares this important tip: "Watch the game film. After any encounter with a manager or coworker, especially one that went particularly well or poorly, review the incident in your mind. Identify what worked, what didn't work, and what you could do better next time."

The truism that age correlates with wisdom is not true in practice. With age comes experience, to be sure, but wisdom, properly understood, is the act of learning from one's experience. Experience happens, but the learning part has always been optional.

Take charge of your own growth toward wisdom by choosing to learn from your experiences, your successes as well as your failures. Create an Incident Log and use it to explore, diagnose, and learn from significant work encounters.

INCIDENT LOG

1. Describe the incident or encounter in your own words.

   _____

   _____

   _____

2. Review your description to look for cases of language that are judging rather than descriptive. (See Chapter 16.) Replace judging language with what you actually saw, heard, or observed.

    _____

    _____

    _____

3. Look for patterns in recent behavior. Was this situation highly unusual or does this happen on a regular basis? (CAUTION: Watch out if you feel this happens *always* or *never*—those are emotionally loaded terms that may indicate the presence of a judging, rather than descriptive, process on your part.)

    _____

    _____

    _____

4. What contributions might you be making to the situation through your own behavior? To what extent could you alter the outcome by changing only your own actions or reactions?

    _____

    _____

    _____

Chapter

49

Develop a Personal Intelligence Network in Your Organization

A large percentage of the staff of the Central Intelligence Agency (CIA) consists of analysts who subscribe to just about every newspaper and magazine in the world, read them, and pull together individual facts, insignificant in themselves, that add up to a revealing whole. Even when the newspapers and magazines are themselves propaganda, and contain content other than the truth, the lies people tell are themselves revealing.

The famous World War II posters warned "Loose Lips Sink Ships." Even if you weren't planning to give away secrets, the smallest details given in the most innocuous settings could be crucial puzzle pieces that enabled the enemy to build a powerful picture.

In your organization, the equivalent items in your "need-to-know" file are such things as upcoming shifts in policy, major changes in the customer base, problems in your competitive environment, critical challenges facing the organization, upcoming shifts in leadership, etc. Forewarned is forearmed, as the saying goes.

It's your turn to be the spy. You need to develop your own organizational CIA, and you can do it ethically, powerfully, and surprisingly easily. Here are some sources of information you need to explore:

Public information. The first step in developing an intelligence network is to identify and evaluate the common, publicly available sources of information.

Is your company publicly held? Buy a minimum of one share of stock, get it held in your name rather than the company's, get the annual reports, and go to the meetings.

Is your company listed in management information resources? Dun & Bradstreet and Standard & Poor are two reference tools that contain valuable data on your company that is often not generally disseminated to employees. Although some of that information is restricted, much of it is available on an open-shelf basis at your local library or on the Internet. Use the Internet to research your company and your industry. If there's a company Web site, check it out.

Read the business section of your newspaper, following not only your company but the local economy and the industry you're in.

Subscribe to trade magazines and journals in your field to keep up with business. If you can wangle invitations to trade shows, go to them and spend any free time researching your competitors and the state of your industry.

Read about your major suppliers as well as your company and its competitors.

Is there a history of your company and your industry in general? Learn about it. You may discover that certain patterns go back generations.

Press information. Your public relations office (marketing or executive if you don't have a separate public relations office) makes a lot of information available to business journalists. You can often get such things as biographies of key executives (a good tool for discovering common interests or background details) and press releases on major events affecting the company. Check with Stockholder Relations as well; they put together lots of information for analysts.

Government information. Especially if you work for a federal or state agency, you can obtain the annual budget, which is public information. In the annual federal budget, for example, there's an appendix that lists changes in the number of authorized positions at each level on the GS (basic federal salary grades) scale. Knowing which departments in your organization are going up or down in head count could put you way ahead of the pack in having time to react.

The rumor mill. Distinguish between gossip, which is largely unprofessional and unproductive, and actual information, which often has a small core of truth in it, even if it's wildly exaggerated. You need to be part of the rumor mill and you need to listen closely, albeit with a grain of salt.

While some experts say you need to share information in order to get it, true gossips really want to be paid for their information in the currency that means the most: good listening. Provide an interested ear, and people will fill it at no extra charge. In fact, being more of a receiver than a distributor of information will help you avoid some of the negative traps involved in rumor mill participation.

Don't believe the majority of what you hear. Listen between the lines. The key secret of good intelligence is to be able to build a pattern out of small bits of information, intuiting an overall structure that enables you to draw meaningful conclusions.

Here's an example of how the spy process works in real life:

I was trying to break into a publishing company even though I didn't have any relevant experience, except that I read and liked their products.

The first thing I did was submit articles to one of their magazines. The pay was nothing, but I was able to have several conversations with the editor by phone.

I learned from him that another contributor to his magazines lived in my city. I called up that person, told him I was a fan of his writing (which actually happened to be true), and offered to take him to lunch. He gave me lots of information about the industry, including some hot rumors about a big license deal that hadn't yet happened.

Armed with this information, I called the company's PR office and told them I was a freelance writer (which was also true). The director of PR spent an hour with me on the phone giving me a history of the company, financial and marketing information, and a packet including bios of all senior company officials. He hinted that the company was shortly planning a big announcement.

I found out about some upcoming hiring plans and was therefore able to submit my resume a few days before the positions became official, meaning I got asked in for the first interview.

In the interview, I noticed a series of boxes containing code names in the manager's office. I put the pieces together: big license deal, upcoming announcement, boxes with code names. "That must be the so-and-so license material," I observed casually, and watched the manager's eyes grow big.

"How did you know?" he asked. I explained the process. "I guess I have to hire you," he laughed. "Can't have that information running around loose."

Notice that these steps are well within the bounds of ethical conduct, and that the knowledge gained was not used in any way harmful to the organization. We call this doing your homework, and it's a good set of policies and rules for you to follow.

If you don't have good information, you can't very well make good decisions.

DEVELOPING YOUR OWN SPY NETWORK

1. What publicly available sources of information cover your company and your industry?

    _____

    _____

    _____

2. What information is supplied to stockholders in general? What information can you obtain on request? What can your broker supply to you in terms of public information and analysis on your company?

    _____

    _____

    _____

3. Who are the people most active in your rumor mill? Which of
    them tends to be most accurate over the long run?

    _____

    _____

    _____

4. Use this information to start a process of gathering nuggets
    of information. Now, begin looking for patterns.

    _____

    _____

    _____

Chapter

Take Care of Your Monkeys, but Don't Collect Them

"**M**onkeys," in the parlance of time and task management, are the problems and issues that pile up on your desk and require your time and attention. Thinking of problems and issues as monkeys helps us remember exactly why they can be such a problem: They require feeding; they make messes; left alone, they tend to get into trouble; they need attention on their schedule, which may not be in tune with your own; and above all, they can breed.

One goal of an effective manager is to get monkeys into the hands of those whose job it is to care for them, which can be tricky for several reasons. One reason is that we often have an innate tendency to take responsibility for any monkey given to us, whether it's ours or not. Another is that we may be frustrated when we think someone isn't taking care of her or his monkey as well (or in the same way) as we would. The result, often, is that when someone comes into our office and asks for advice on his or her monkey, we end up with one more monkey swinging around the office making messes.

A manager who is aware of the monkey situation knows that when a subordinate comes into the office saying, "I don't know what to do with my monkey!" the goal is first to help the subordinate take the next step, and second to have the subordinate leave carrying the monkey.

The situation is somewhat different when you are the subordinate. It is part of your job and your responsibility to take responsibility for your own monkeys and not to burden your supervisor unfairly, but it is also important for you to know when the monkeys aren't yours and what to do with them then.

Taking Responsibility for Your Own Monkeys

Monkeys come in different sizes. In other words, your efforts to identify your own critical priorities help you determine which monkeys come first, which get fed, and which get put aside until later.

The problem comes up either when you don't know how to take care of a particular monkey or when you don't have the authority necessary to take care of that monkey. In both cases, you may need to involve your boss.

When you need information and ideas. If you don't know how to care for a particular monkey, you may need training or skill development, or you may simply need advice or a tip on what to do next. It's appropriate—indeed, it's often necessary—to go to your boss on such matters. To be a good subordinate, make sure you communicate clearly and up front that you're not trying to give away the monkey, but instead to get the knowledge and advice necessary to do the work yourself.

Check to see if your boss is the right person to help you. Perhaps a coworker or other colleague is a better choice. Can you get the necessary information through reading, reference, or other outside sources?

When you need authority. If you don't have the necessary authority or decision-making range, then you're in a situation in which upward delegation isn't boss abuse—it's necessary. Your boss exists in part to take certain upwardly delegated assignments from subordinates, primarily those that require decisions and authority grants above a certain level.

If you don't have the authority or decision power, then you have to delegate those matters upward in the chain of command. That's not sloughing off your responsibility; that's performing it properly. Take a look at your monkeys and key responsibilities. Where are the limits of your authority and power? What decisions and steps are necessary to the completion of your assignment that only your boss can do?

To delegate upward in a proper manner, you need to bring most issues to your boss in a timely manner that allows the opportunity for review and thought before a decision must be made. There will, of course, be times when that's not possible, but when you've provided the thinking option most of the time, you'll get a better response when you can't provide the option. Identify what you need, when you need it, and the consequences that will result.

Don't exaggerate or build up the latter; tell the truth. But if you need a decision by close of business on Thursday or else the project will fail at a cost of half a million dollars, it's certainly appropriate—indeed, essential—to let your boss know. In that situation, putting it in writing would also be smart. Using urgency and consequences to compel a boss's decision may be tempting, especially if you've got a boss who is otherwise slow or reluctant to decide, but you don't want to acquire a reputation as "the boy who cried 'wolf!' "

Refusing to Care for Someone Else's Monkey

We want to be team players and cooperative employees, but that doesn't mean it's right or proper to accept responsibility for monkeys on a wholesale basis. We have our own essential responsibilities, as others do, and knowing when—and how—to say no to assignments you shouldn't take is an important strategy.

Know when to say no. The more you have a clear sense of your own professional priorities and obligations, the easier it is to say no to obligations that properly aren't yours. You have only a certain amount of time, and whenever you do what you shouldn't be doing, you necessarily aren't doing what you should be doing.

Know how to say no. This book has already shown you different techniques to say no, especially when you're overloaded on higher-priority work. Make sure you avoid a related problem, which is making someone angry or resentful during the process of saying no.

To avoid—or at least lessen—the problem, you can use a powerful technique: Say no to the job, not the person. When people hear a negative, they may take the rejection personally. But you don't have to reject a person in order to reject the task or assignment that person wants you to accept. As consultant Dave Gustafson observes, "Ever been trapped by a smooth or fast-talking coworker who drops a few pearls and quick ideas here and there, then suggests you take the action (while they take the credit)? Just say, 'You've given this serious thought. Let me think it over and I'll get back to you.' Putting some time in between may lessen the pressure from the coworker, it will give you time to think about whether taking on the job is really the right thing for you, and it may help you think of other options.''

QUICK TIP SELF-ASSESSMENT

1. Do I know which monkeys are really mine and which belong to other people? Am I successful in not taking monkeys that don't belong to me?

    _____

    _____

    _____

2. In my current project and task list, what information or technical answers do I need but don't have right now? What is the best way for me to get them?

    _____

    _____

    _____

3. What decisions or permissions on my current project and task list need to be performed by my boss? How can I best inform my boss of the necessary actions and their time requirements and consequences?

    _____

    _____

    _____

4. If I'm frequently taking monkeys that don't belong to me, do I have a problem saying no? What are some ways I can more easily reject and refuse assignments that should go to someone else?

    _____

    _____

    _____

Chapter

Identify and Go After
Important Job Assignments

As you've learned, demonstrating initiative is one of the most powerful techniques for career advancement in general, and managing your boss in particular. Ultimately, if you don't add to your own set of responsibilities, your job title and pay are unlikely to change dramatically.

Job assignments are not equal. Some assignments carry with them far greater intrinsic and extrinsic rewards. Some assignments allow you to acquire new skills, build an expanded network of contacts, become visible to those in the upper reaches of the organization, and add measurable accomplishments to your performance appraisal and résumé. Other assignments may be necessary, but don't advance your long-term interests in any particular respect.

You've got to do both types of assignments in any job, but doing more of the first will clearly do more for you.

Earn the Right to Be Considered for
Career-Advancing Assignments

The best assignments—the ones that lead to advancement—are never distributed in an equal manner. A variety of criteria go into management decisions.

Positive behaviors that get good assignments. The first, of course, is experience. Two people may have equal ability in theory, but the one who's done it successfully before has an edge.

The second is overall attitude. The person who is generally reluctant to take on new assignments, or has a track record of complaining, is less likely to be picked.

Related to overall attitude is the attitude with which the person does assignments that are not considered career advancing. If you get a reputation for being willing to do great assignments but being unwilling to put in your time in the trenches, you may find that those great assignments go elsewhere.

A third reason is track record. When you've successfully completed an important assignment, you're more likely to get a chance at another.

Negative behaviors that get good assignments—and how to counter them. Some negative behaviors have been known to work, at least on a short-term basis. Operating on the management principle "the squeaky wheel gets the grease," some people campaign for good assignments and reject less beneficial ones through a nonstop campaign of aggressive whining.

The trick is that in order for the negative behavior to work, the other people in the department have to collaborate in letting it work. It normally takes a lack of assertiveness and campaigning behavior on the part of others for this strategy to succeed. You might be reluctant to campaign on the grounds that you don't want to be thought of as that sort of person. On the other hand, it's been demonstrated that management awards good job assignments at least in part on the basis of campaigning; therefore, you must campaign as well.

Develop good assignments for yourself. Not all the best assignments are determined by your boss and others in management. There are normally some important and critical job assignments that you can essentially create on your own.

When you bring forward a new job assignment, including a plan for how to deal with it successfully (while, of course, keeping up with your current job responsibilities), you automatically become the leading candidate for the position.

QUICK TIP SELF-ASSESSMENT

1. What job assignments would be most beneficial to my career and organizational goals?

    _____

    _____

    _____

2. How can I demonstrate my suitability in terms of skills, attitude, and appropriate self-promotion?

    _____

    _____

    _____

3. What important and valuable job assignments can I create for myself to lead toward the goals I want to accomplish?

    _____

    _____

    _____

Chapter

52

Learn How to Delegate

We've observed that a lack of delegation skills is the number one reason why managers fail. What's less obvious, though equally true, is that poor delegation skills are a key reason why almost anyone in the world of work can fail.

Delegation is the act of getting someone to take on part of your responsibility and giving him or her a sufficient grant of authority to do that work. And everyone needs to delegate, regardless of position in the organization hierarchy. You don't even need to be a manager or have staff in order to delegate.

Think about it this way: Could you possibly get your own work done without the willing and voluntary cooperation of a number of people over whom you have no direct authority or power whatsoever? For most people, the answer is "No!" And an enormous amount of frustration and pain result from the conflict between the power you have and the power you need to get the work done.

Let's face it. You can't get the work done without the cooperation of others. They can't get their work done without that cooperation either. We're pretty much all in the same boat.

There are a number of reasons people have trouble delegating. If you're not a manager, perhaps the number one problem you are experiencing is not having anyone to delegate to. If you don't have staff, how can you delegate?

The answer is simple if you take a wide enough view of what it means to delegate.

People You Can Delegate to

You can always find someone to whom you can delegate. Let's look at some of the resources available within your own organization right now:

People to Whom You Can Delegate	Description
The Delegator	This is the person who gave you a legitimate decision. Take the opportunity to negotiate. Yes, you can delegate to someone who's trying to delegate to you—the strategy is, "I'll be glad to do this if you'll help."
Your Management Chain	This is your boss and others above you in the chain of command. Certain decisions and approvals must be made at higher levels.
The Attempted Delegator	This is the person who tries to delegate an inappropriate task or project. The goal is to say no effectively.
Colleagues/Same Level	These are the people at your own organizational level. You need to win their cooperation to achieve your goals.
Temporary Coverage	This occurs when you travel, take vacation, or just go to lunch. It's about arranging temporary pick-up of your responsibilities during your absence.
Staff	These are the traditional people to whom you delegate. You should delegate to them; you just shouldn't stop there.
Outsiders	These are subcontractors, other departments, service professionals. They make their living by taking on your delegations.

These categories cover just about everyone, and just about everyone fits into the realm of people to whom you can delegate.

Delegating to the delegator. The person who gives you delegations, be it boss or colleague or customer, may also need to provide you with assistance and support along with the assignment. "I'll be glad to do it, if you'll help," you say, and then specify the type of help and assistance you need. You can take part of a delegated assignment and not the whole. You can take an assignment contingent on getting certain resources or staff support. You can postpone your acceptance of the assignment until you've had time to think it through, to identify issues requiring explanation, support, or change. You can negotiate a different project from the one originally proposed. You can take on this assignment by removing that assignment from your schedule (or postponing it or lowering its priority). All these possibilities exist.

Note that your leverage to get some of these changes tends to be higher before you've said yes. Once you agree to the assignment, you're comparatively locked in, not only to the assignment itself, but to the hidden assumptions, agendas, and circumstances you might not have considered or known about.

Your management chain. "Upward delegation" tends to be shorthand for boss abuse, manipulative employee behavior that managers are taught to avoid. But as we've seen, your boss has certain duties and responsibilities that properly originate at the staff level and flow upward. You not only can delegate upward in certain circumstances, you should and you must.

Examples of situations calling for legitimate upward delegation include decisions that are out of your purview, situations in which managerial signature authority is necessary, and conflicts with other assignments and priorities.

In addition, there are situations in which your boss's leverage can solve problems and reduce your workload and effort. For example, if you're having trouble getting cooperation from another department, it may be more effective to ask your boss to run interference for you or negotiate the support you need rather than hit your head against the wall.

Dealing with an attempted delegation. Sometimes the right answer to a delegated assignment is, "Thanks for the opportunity, but why don't you do it or get someone else to do it?" While you obviously need to be careful about when and how to refuse job assignments, there's an appropriate place for this.

Most offices have a person chock full of ideas who is missing the follow-through. "I've got a great idea," comes the enthusiastic refrain, which is followed by the search for the victim. That person will do the work, but of course the idea creator, like the friends of the little red hen, will be there waiting for a full share of the credit.

Sometimes, it's vital that you say no even to legitimate work assignments because you're working on something with so much greater priority that something's got to give.

Delegating to colleagues and others at your level. An enormous amount of delegation happens among people who are at roughly the same organizational level. You probably take at least some of your delegated assignments from coworkers now. It's important to be aware of the systematic process for which it happens.

Why and under what circumstances will you take an assignment from a coworker? There are many possibilities.

- You have special skills.
- You currently have the time.
- It's your area of responsibility.
- The assignment was given to the wrong person in the first place, and you're the right person.
- You're a team player and this is a team.
- You like being helpful and supportive.
- You figure that now they owe you one.

All these reasons are perfectly legitimate. They're also the reasons others may be willing to take on assignments you delegate to them.

The key difference in this sort of delegation is that you have to ask them to take on the assignment because you don't have the official power to demand that they do so. In fact, this isn't that much different from delegating to anyone else. The mere fact that you may possess the technical authority to compel someone's obedience doesn't mean it's a smart idea to use that power when it's not necessary.

The steps in a good delegation are:

- *Determine* exactly what you need.
- *Explain* the assignment carefully, including timing issues.
- *Identify* the importance, priority, and potential benefits.
- *Provide* the necessary resources and authority.
- *Ask* for the cooperation and help.
- *Follow up* to provide support and monitor performance.

Temporary coverage. Have you ever experienced the problem of someone going on vacation or travel without arranging for coverage for her or his responsibility, leaving you stuck, unable to complete a key assignment because that person had the information and resources you needed?

If you have, then you know how important it is to arrange coverage and support for your absences. Clearly, it's good for you—but it's also good for everyone else in your department, from the boss on down.

Arranging coverage can be as simple as the secretary who announces, "Who's going to cover the phones when I'm at lunch?" or as complex as preparing a formal memo listing your ongoing responsibilities and contact people for your absences.

A good professional technique is to prepare a standard coverage document that can be tweaked slightly for each absence. The document should include who will make necessary and unpostponable decisions related to your responsibilities in your absence, where key information is located, a list of major current projects and the status of each, and any on-the-road contact information it may be appropriate to provide. Set your e-mail to give a bounce-back message so people know if you will not be able to reply on a normal schedule; prepare a voice mail message giving information on whom to talk to in your absence.

Staff. Numerous volumes go into great detail on how to be an effective delegator to your staff, and we don't need to repeat that here. Please note that most of the same techniques that will make you a better staff delegator will also improve your ability to delegate to the others mentioned here.

The most common reason people give for not delegating is the refrain, "I can do it better/faster/cheaper/etc., myself!" Of course, this statement is frequently true. That's a big part of the reason you're where you are right now. But were you that good when you started? Most of us were not. We learned through doing, and worked to develop our skills to their current level.

What we often forget is that there are two separate reasons for you to delegate an assignment. The first reason, of course, is to free you up for other work that only you can do. In that case, you need to find someone who is capable and willing to do the work well enough that you don't have to stand over his or her shoulder.

The other reason to delegate, however, is different. Delegation is the most common form of on-the-job training in most organizations. It's the way people learn by doing. Of course, if you're delegating for the purpose of training, then it shouldn't surprise you that you'll have to spend more time and more energy to get a result that takes longer and is likely poorer than what you could have done on your own. That's perfectly normal; that's the training and learning process that all human beings go through.

Improve your organizational effectiveness by resolving to take some of your assignments that right now no one but you can do and "delegate for turnover." That means to provide the training, support, and encouragement over time to help someone grow and develop to the point that they can take on the assignment and make it their own.

And don't worry about your job security if you do this. There's an old saying, "If you're so good that you can't be replaced, you can't very well be promoted, either." It's not the jobs you know how to do that make you secure in a job; it's the overall skill, versatility, and growth potential you have.

Delegating out. People make their living by taking on your delegated assignments, and because they do nothing but those assignments, sometimes delegating out is economically superior to doing it yourself, even when cash is involved.

The trick is to determine what your time is worth and what you would do productively with that time if only you could unload some specific responsibilities. If the value of the time saved exceeds the cost of time saved, it's a smart move.

What's the Value of Your Time?

Your Salary	Value of a Minute	Value of an Hour	Value of Saving an Hour a Day for a Week	Value of Saving an Hour a Day for a Year
$ 15,000.00	$0.13	$ 7.81	$ 39.06	$ 1,875.00
20,000.00	0.17	10.42	52.08	2,500.00
30,000.00	0.26	15.63	78.13	3,750.00
40,000.00	0.35	20.83	104.17	5,000.00
60,000.00	0.52	31.25	156.25	7,500.00
80,000.00	0.69	41.67	208.33	10,000.00
100,000.00	0.87	52.08	260.42	12,500.00

You can delegate, regardless of your organizational or hierarchical position. There's always someone who can take on assignments and projects for you, if you ask clearly, nicely, and assertively.

DELEGATION EFFECTIVENESS

1. Make a list of all the people to whom you can at least in theory delegate, using the categories in this section.

    _____

    _____

2. What are the tasks, projects, and issues that you have that can potentially be delegated, either in whole or in part?

    _____

    _____

3. Who would be the best people for those jobs?

    _____

    _____

4. How could you organize and prepare for your delegations to encourage others to accept those responsibilities from you?

    _____

    _____

5. How would you benefit from the extra time available for other tasks and projects?

    _____

    _____

6. What benefits would the organization as a whole (and your department specifically) gain from your success in delegating?

    _____

    _____

Chapter

53

Don't Try to Manipulate;
Try to Influence, Instead

There's a difference between manipulation and influence, although the two are often confused in both theory and practice.

Manipulation. Manipulation techniques tend to leave the victim
unaware or helpless. If you play on someone's sense of insecurity in
order to motivate certain behavior, that's manipulation. The person
may not be consciously aware what has happened.

Influence. Influence techniques still allow the person on whom
they are used to make a choice. If you deliver a convincing argument, if you identify the benefits that will result from doing it your
way, if you offer to negotiate, and if you communicate in a persuasive way, the recipient of your influence still has the conscious
power to choose whether to agree, cooperate, or go along.

It's still influence—not manipulation—even if the other choice
is a poor one. In fact, alternatives frequently aren't exactly equal.
"We can go ahead with the plan, or we can lose a million dollars.
It's your choice." That's still perfectly fair behavior, as long as your
presentation of the alternatives is honest and complete.

Problems with manipulation. Using manipulative behavior has a
number of problems and disadvantages.

The first problem is ethics. While not all forms of manipulation are inherently unethical, you're at least skirting the line. Because the key characteristics of manipulation are that the person is either unaware or helpless in the face of the manipulative behavior, you're attempting to deprive someone of choice.

The second problem is skill. Frankly, it takes skill to be a successful manipulator, and the office is full of people whose track record is spotty, at best. It's bad enough to be a skilled manipulator, but the unskilled manipulator (or semiskilled manipulator) comes in for more than her or his share of negative reactions. The fundamental rule is that if people catch you at it, you're not very good—and you will pay.

The third problem is persistence. As the saying goes, "A man convinced against his will / Is of his own opinion still." Unless your need for someone's cooperation or support is of a short-term nature, you'll often find that manipulation wears off too quickly. You've had the experience of being manipulated into certain behavior or feelings, only to come back to your senses an hour or so later, feeling angry and used.

The fourth problem is resistance. Once you're known as someone who regularly uses manipulative behavior, others tend to become progressively resistant—they become immunized to the disease. Although you can find people who remain susceptible, they become fewer and fewer.

The fifth problem is revenge. When people come to the realization that they have been manipulated, their reaction is not positive. You may find that, out of spite, people tend to resist or even sabotage your desires or interests.

Developing influence skills. The rules for developing influence are similar to the rules for developing and gaining power. Review the Four R's: Role, Respect, Relationships, and Rhetoric. How can you expand your success in these four critical areas?

On a situational level, you can increase your case-by-case influence through a fifth R: Research. Your persuasiveness on an issue or behavior can be improved by the quality of your analysis and the quality of your argument. Are your facts straight? Is your understanding sound? And have you fully considered the interests and ideas of those who disagree? The last step, too often overlooked, is crucial because changing the understanding of those who disagree is the goal of influence. If you don't understand where they're coming from or where they are, there's little likelihood of moving elsewhere.

Advantages of an influence strategy. Because influence strategies are by their nature aboveboard and allow choice on the part of the recipient (even if the choice is limited), such strategies avoid most of the problems associated with manipulative behavior.

First, the behavior is clearly ethical. When you don't try to trick people or deprive them of choice, there's nothing questionable in the behavior. Second, cases in which you lack the necessary skill to achieve the desired influence don't rebound on you the next time you try. Third, when influence strategies succeed, they tend to succeed for the long term. Fourth, influence doesn't build up resistance in its targets. Fifth, the desire for revenge doesn't result.

QUICK TIP SELF-ASSESSMENT

1. What are the current strengths and weaknesses in my influence skills?

   _____

   _____

2. How can I leverage my "Four R" power to increase my ability to influence others in appropriate ways?

   _____

   _____

3. Where can my "Fifth R"—Research—provide me with the tools I need to achieve my influence goals?

   _____

   _____

4. Are there manipulation techniques I use now that I should try to avoid in the future?

   _____

   _____

Chapter

54

Uncover Hidden Agendas

As you have probably already realized, the real reason something is done is often different from the official reason. The real reason is known as the hidden agenda, and hidden agendas are the bane of many in the organization.

"That person has a hidden agenda." We're all aware that hidden agendas exist—perhaps even predominate—in the workplace. Simply put, hidden agendas are people's unstated goals and objectives. Sometimes, the hidden agenda is so hidden that it's a subconscious motivation on the part of the person with the agenda!

Among the many problems with the hidden agenda is that the very name tends to fill us with a sense of helplessness. No matter how much we need to know about it, if an agenda is "hidden," doesn't that make us helpless?

Fortunately, the answer is a clear "No."

Ways to Uncover Hidden Agendas

The only characteristic that makes a hidden agenda "hidden" is that you are unaware what it is. To turn it around, all you have to do is discover it. Let's look at some ways you can do this.

Assume there's one there. The first tip for uncovering a hidden agenda is to assume that there is indeed one present. A number of people go into complex organizational issues without taking the time to think about whether one or more of the participants has an agenda—until it's too late. Just assume hidden agendas are at work until and unless you determine otherwise.

Put yourself in their shoes. That someone has a hidden agenda is an elaborate way of saying he or she has a goal or interest that is not clearly on the table for discussion. Perhaps that person's career or organizational interests will be advanced or retarded by the issue at hand.

Put yourself in the other person's shoes and try to imagine the situation from that point of view. Be on the lookout for potentially embarrassing consequences your project could have for others in the organization.

Ask them directly. It's surprising, but a number of agendas remain hidden only because we didn't actually ask about them. "How will this affect you or your organizational interests?" may well reveal critical information.

The reason is that hidden agendas are not always synonymous with "secret" agendas. There may not be a conspiracy to keep the information from you; it's just that people don't always think to share. They may even assume you already know, and become angry with you for what seems to them to be deliberate sabotage of their interests, when the truth is that communication never took place at all.

Here's a simple, powerful, direct method that will frequently provide information of value. "I've been asked to look into this matter, so I thought the best thing to do was to ask you if you had issues, concerns, or other plans, before I actually go ahead and do anything that might cause a problem."

Ask someone else who might know. If you're having trouble uncovering a hidden agenda by putting yourself in another's shoes and asking directly doesn't work or seems politically unwise, find someone else who might know. "Is there anything I should know about the interests and goals of the players in this situation?" may give you a surprising amount of information.

If you feel it is uncomfortable or unwise for you to approach the vice president of another division, for example, you can ask someone you know in that division, or ask your boss for background or help in making the contact.

Learn from experience. Most of us have suffered through various organizational embarrassments. Make sure you use such disasters as learning experiences if they can't be avoided. Your career will probably not be too damaged from a single disaster. But if you start another major project without determining the presence of a political minefield, you'll become known as someone who doesn't learn very well. That would be a real failure.

Quick Tip Self-Assessment

1. Who are the people who can be affected, positively and negatively, by my projects?

    _____

    _____

2. By putting myself in their shoes and looking at the situation from their perspective, what can I learn about their likely agenda and issues?

    _____

    _____

3. How can I ask them directly, or ask others who may know, to identify any agenda items?

    _____

    _____

4. What do my previous experiences in the organization suggest about potential hidden agendas here?

    _____

    _____

5. How can I address the needs and concerns of the hidden agendas so I can lower the political tension and stakes surrounding my projects?

    _____

    _____

Chapter

55

Build Connections With Other Departments

A major government agency was building a new building, expected to be a showcase example of efficiency. There were the normal problems on the project, of course. One critical problem had to do with procurement.

In private industry, the job of the procurement or purchasing function is basically to buy what the departments need. In government, the procurement function has a primary responsibility to see that the laws and regulations governing purchases are enforced— and then to buy what the departments need.

It's obviously necessary to have these regulations to avoid the appearance—or actuality—of impropriety, but the regulations come at a cost: They make purchasing more complex, and in some cases hamper the departments' ability to get what they need when they need it.

Limits of Position Power

The application of position power—rank—is normally not enough to change things. If the head of the agency gets into a fight with a procurement clerk over the regulations, there's a good chance the head of the agency will have to give in. The clerk isn't just a clerk, but rather an enforcer of the law. (That doesn't mean you can't use position power to compel or urge people to play fast and loose with the regulations; it's done all the time. However, it's done at a price, even when you're very powerful, and there are potential consequences that don't apply at all outside the governmental sphere.)

It's also the case that the people in procurement can be more aggressive or less aggressive in enforcing the details of the regulations, and put your work first—or last—in the stack. What they lack in the power of their job title, they gain instead in the power of the regulations. They don't have to commit sabotage; merely refraining from giving top effort will be enough to cause enormous damage to the completion of this building project.

The problem is that failure is not an option. For the project head to complain that the building was late because the procurement clerks wouldn't cooperate would be an embarrassment. It just wouldn't fly. Yet the problem is very real.

When your job depends on your relationships with other departments, and you don't have direct authority over them, you're in a very vulnerable position indeed.

What Would You Do?

What would you do if you were in charge of this project?

It's obvious that you need cheerful and above-the-call-of-duty cooperation and support from the procurement team. It's equally obvious you can't force it. Here's what the executive in charge actually did.

She started by picking a person from each of the divisions to be the procurement liaison for his or her division, and called these people into her office. "I've made arrangements for you to get a tour and orientation of the procurement operation tomorrow," she announced. "Here's some money to take them to lunch. Your job is to come back and give me some ideas on how we can be of better service to them."

One of the group raised his hand. "I don't understand. I thought their job was to be of service to us."

The executive just smiled and reconfirmed her order.

The next day, she called the group in again. "Well," she said, "what did you learn?"

The person who'd spoken up the previous day was the first one to speak. "Ma'am, they hate us over there."

The executive nodded thoughtfully. "That's interesting. What makes you think that?"

"Well, I kept asking how we could help them, like you said. And finally one of them got quite angry and said, 'You want to know how you can help us? You people in the line departments don't have a clue, do you? We're spending nearly half our time re-doing paperwork that's supposed to be right when it comes to us in the first place!'"

"What do you think we ought to do about that?" the executive said.

"I think we ought to learn to fill out the forms correctly, if that's such a big deal!"

The executive smiled, for on her desk were the documents to enroll each member of the group in the introductory training program for procurement professionals.

Getting Cooperative Results From Other Departments

What are the likely results from this effort? First, the forms will be right when they go over. Second, after a while (people have to get used to being treated well), they'll start to expect forms from that group to be right, and do them first, because they're easy.

Third, they'll be far more willing to take the extra steps that are necessary, because they will feel supported. Fourth, while they won't break the law or regulations, there are inevitably situations that call for judgment. Those judgment calls can go for or against the group. Now, they're more likely to go in the positive and desired direction.

Understanding Other Functions

In working with other departments effectively, the first rule is to improve your understanding of that department's needs and objectives. If you can't see it from their point of view, you won't understand why it is they don't rush forward to meet all your needs.

Understanding involves two aspects: empathy, or seeing the emotional stress as they see it; and literal understanding, knowing the processes and problems others experience. You can't very well have a good working relationship with another department within your organization if you don't have a good idea what that department does, what its needs and objectives are, what its problems are, and how you can be of service. Build emotional, or empathetic, listening on a foundation of actual understanding.

That understanding is mutually beneficial. Not only does your understanding of their problems and issues improve their lives (and thereby your relationship) but it also expands your knowledge of the organization, which may be of continuing benefit in your own advancement.

Executives, regardless of their organizational origin, are necessarily generalists, because a wide understanding of the different needs that exist within the organization is vital.

Treating Other Departments as Customers

Understanding is the first key; treating other departments like customers is the second key. Quality expert Joseph Jablonski reminds us, "[W]e acknowledge the existence of many customers we may have overlooked in the past. This includes the customer outside an organization, the big C. In addition, there is a little 'c,' the customers within our company with whom we work on a daily basis. . . . We relate well to the big C, but our support and enthusiasm often wane when we support the little c's. This frequently results from our indirect compensation for these services."[47]

But we do pay, and sometimes pay and pay and pay, when the relationship is bad. Your customers are everyone you depend on for the resources that let you get your work done.

Building Personal Relationships

The third key is that people do favors for those they like and withhold favors from those they don't like.

In the building project, getting good results from procurement began as a process of providing customer service and support through correct and timely paperwork and awareness of and support for the regulatory responsibilities that the procurement office had. But it didn't stop there.

"These people are part of our team," the executive told her procurement liaisons. "Let's treat them that way." When T-shirts were made up for team members, the procurement specialists got some. When there was a party held for team members, the procurement specialists were invited. When the grand opening party was held (a hot Washington ticket), the procurement specialists got to go.

47. Jablonski, Joseph. *Implementing Total Quality Management: An Overview.* San Diego, Calif.: Pfeiffer & Co., 1991, pp. 25–26.

The Farleyfile

According to science fiction writer (and one-time political candidate) Robert A. Heinlein, the most valuable political tool ever invented was the Farleyfile, named for Eisenhower's campaign manager, who invented the device. Basically, the Farleyfile consisted of a record of everyone the candidate met, no matter how briefly, along with every bit of information, no matter how trivial: "names and nicknames of wives, children, and pets, hobbies, tastes in food or drink [and] date and place and comments for *every occasion* [emphasis added] on which [the candidate] had talked to that particular man."[48]

He comments, "The point is that top-level men like [the President] meet many more people than they can remember. Each one of that faceless throng remembers his own meeting with the famous man and remembers it in detail. But the supremely important person in any one's life is *himself* [emphasis added]—and a politician must never forget that."

A simple technique for making your own Farleyfile is to get in the habit of keeping your Rolodex open whenever you talk to someone, even if you have his or her phone number memorized. When a personal detail comes up that you might otherwise tend to forget, jot it down. You'll get a reputation for being thoughtful and considerate, and a reputation like that will go a very long way.

48. Heinlein, Robert A. *Double Star*. Signet/New American Library: New York, 1957, pp. 81–83.

WORKING WITH OTHER DEPARTMENTS

1. Where am I dependent on other people and other departments without direct authority to compel my objectives?

    _____

    _____

    _____

2. What is the level of cooperation and support I get from those departments? In what ways is it satisfactory, and in what ways is it lacking?

    _____

    _____

    _____

3. How can I gain a full understanding of the issues and problems that concern those on whom I am dependent? How can I help them?

    _____

    _____

    _____

4. In what ways can I provide bonuses and incentives to improve cooperation and support?

    _____

    _____

    _____

5. What steps can I take to build better personal relationships in support of my goals?

    _____

    _____

    _____

Chapter

56

Identify Your Boss's Allies and Enemies to Avoid Stepping on the Wrong Toes

Because you represent your boss, your boss's enemies and allies will to some extent act toward you as they would toward your boss. Sometimes this means that you find others reacting to you in ways your own conduct doesn't warrant. At other times, you discover to your embarrassment that simply being friendly to the wrong person lands you in hot water with your boss.

While it is possible to have different allies and enemies than your boss, it's vital to know your boss's political landscape as well as you know your own. As Speaker Tip O'Neill puts it, "Remember your friends, and who their enemies are, too."[49]

Recognizing Your Boss's Allies and Enemies

Allies and enemies exist in the organizational framework for a variety of reasons. Look at the individual reasons as they might apply to your boss (or yourself, or indeed anyone you want or need to analyze) and determine who fits into the specific categories.

49. O'Neill, Tip. Op. cit., p. 107.

Structural. An old Defense Department joke says that the real enemy of the U.S. Army was never the former Soviet Union—it was, and is, the U.S. Navy, and vice versa. Interservice, interagency, or interdepartmental alliances and rivalries occur when interests and goals are in alignment or in opposition. Sometimes your enemies and your allies occupy those positions because the departments tend naturally to be at loggerheads.

One common source of tension is when departments handle a project in sequence order; that is, one department does its portion of the work, then hands it to the next department in the age-old technique known as "throwing it over the wall."

Because interim deadlines are inherently more flexible than final deadlines, the first departments in the sequence find it easier to be late with their work. As the process advances, the pressure to make up the lost time increases, until the final department in line ends up taking the brunt of the consequences for all the previous lateness in the system. Resentment, as you can imagine, is virtually inevitable.

Resources. When two or more projects or departments compete for resources (budget, people, or tools), conflict is likely. Both sides have a basic incentive to use the political tools of the unofficial organization to get their way. The situation turns personal when one side perceives the other isn't playing fair, especially if that side is also perceived as winning disproportionately.

The old saying goes, "Never leave a wounded enemy on the field of battle with the incentive to return and take revenge." This leads back to the necessity for win/win negotiation, but when that has not previously been the tradition, problems are likely.

Personal. Political biographer Robert Caro writes: "There is an expression used in [New York State politics] to describe the relationship of two men between whom there exists bad feeling when that feeling has existed for years, has resisted every attempt at reconciliation and has only deepened with the passage of time, to a point where 'dislike' is not so fitting a name for it as 'hatred.' In discussing two such men, one assemblyman will say to another, with a knowing shake of his head: 'They go back a long way.' "[50]

When your boss and someone else in the management structure "go back a long way," that's something to watch out for. When enmity is deep enough and long lasting enough, the people who are

50. Caro, Robert A. *The Power Broker: Robert Moses and the Fall of New York.* New York: Alfred A. Knopf, 1974, p. 283.

involved in the feud may well take steps that aren't even in their own best interests just to do damage to someone else.

Take the time to study who the allies and enemies are of your boss and others in the management structure, because those interpersonal relationships can have a dramatic and very negative effect on your own fortunes.

QUICK TIP SELF-ASSESSMENT

1. Who are the people and departments that are generally allied with my boss personally and my department or project generally?

_____

_____

_____

2. Who are the people and departments that are generally opposed to the interests of my boss personally and my department or project generally?

_____

_____

_____

3. In the case of enemies of my boss, what is the origin of the enmity?

_____

_____

_____

4. How should I manage my relationships with my boss's allies and enemies?

_____

_____

_____

Chapter

57

Ask for a Promotion

Here's another true story:

Our company was in the throes of massive layoffs, the result of poor financial results and pressure from the banks. In fact, we lost nearly 75 percent of our workforce in five rounds of layoffs—and I had no seniority! In fact, I had been there only six months, and had relocated to take the job to boot.

There was only one thing I could think of to do: I went to the vice president of my group and asked him to lunch. This was a little dangerous; he was three levels above me. But he accepted.

At lunch, I told him that I believed the company would turn around, that I was interested in being part of that effort, and that I wanted him to consider me for extra responsibilities or advancement when the opportunity arose.

He looked at me as if I were completely nuts, but less than a month later, he came into my cubicle. "I'm laying off the entire marketing department this week. How would you like to take their place?"

And that's how I became the marketing manager for a $20 million company.

Does this sound completely insane? It's not; in fact, it's an extreme but useful example of a powerful strategy that ought to be part of your own program for managing up.

Initiative, we've learned, is a job qualifier. So is interest. It's reasonable to believe that, other things being equal, someone who wants additional responsibility will do better with it rather than someone who's reluctant. That means there are many people who actually want a promotion or job advancement or additional responsibility who don't get it—because they don't actually ask for it. People assume they aren't really interested, and give the opportunity to someone who clearly is.

Second, promotions are normally after-the-fact affairs. Many people report their enormous frustration and anger because they're asked to take on substantial additional responsibilities without getting the title and pay that go along with it. It's more useful to look at that as an audition for promotion, because quite often the title (and pay) will come along some time later—normally, after you've proven yourself in your new responsibilities.

Make it clear that you want advancement, that you want additional responsibilities, that you're actively looking for a promotion, if indeed that is your goal. You've heard it said many times, "If you don't ask, you don't get." That's very true, not because people necessarily want to withhold what you want, but because they don't actually know what it is you want in the first place.

QUICK TIP SELF-ASSESSMENT

1. Have I made it actively clear that I'm looking for career advancement or promotion?

    _____

    _____

    _____

2. Have I made it clear to the right people—those who can do something about it? If not, how can I reach them to make my interest known?

    _____

    _____

    _____

3. How am I demonstrating in my current position that I have
    the interest and desire for more?

    _____

    _____

    _____

4. Have I shown a willingness to take on new roles even if I
    haven't been offered the title and pay—and to regard it as an
    audition, not a punishment?

    _____

    _____

    _____

Chapter

58

Deal Effectively With Stereotypes and Prejudices

We've talked extensively about networking and relationship building within the unofficial organization of the workplace. This unofficial power structure is known as the "old boy network," and it is legitimately an area of concern for those who don't fit the standard picture or criteria for membership.

Mike Duncan, vice president for personnel for a $25 billion corporation and an expert in the challenges that African Americans, in particular, face in the workplace, observes, "The 'old boy network' is a serious problem for most African American employees who are trying to get ahead. The problem is not so much that such a phenomenon exists; the problem is knowing how to manage yourself for peak effectiveness in spite of the old boy syndrome, and also knowing what knowledge you need for protection."[51]

You may have special challenges in managing up because of gender, racial, cultural, religious, or other categories to which you belong. The bad news is that problems clearly exist. The good news, however, is that people achieve advancement and good results every

51. Duncan, Mike. *Reach Your Goals in Spite of the Old Boy Network: A Guide for African American Employees*. Edgewood, Md.: Duncan & Duncan, 1990, p. 10.

day in spite of the real obstacles they face as a result of gender or ethnic or racial discrimination. By analyzing the situation and developing action tools, you can beat the odds and achieve your career goals.

The barriers to your success and advancement can be grouped into two rough classifications: those that apply to all employees and those that apply either uniquely or more stringently to employees who are women or minorities.

Let's face it: It's tough for just about everybody, regardless of status or classification. That's why it's important not to confuse a general mistreatment of employees with racial or sexual discrimination. "I don't discriminate—I mistreat and humiliate everyone equally!" is, unfortunately, the behavior practiced by some bosses.

General Barriers to Advancement

Although general barriers to advancement, such as the hotel initiative test described previously, basically operate without deliberately intended discrimination, they often end up having discriminatory effects.

The reason is that to surmount these barriers often takes having someone sit you down and explain the game to you; in other words, you need to get good mentoring. Because mentors take under their wings those who remind them of themselves, for the most part, a white male "old boy" structure is inherently friendlier to young white males of similar social class, education, and culture.

Duncan observes, "There are very few Blacks that can advance and maintain their status without a solid support group. As a matter of fact, there are few Whites who can make it without strong support from a variety of other people."[52] Denise Dudley believes the same strategy applies to women: "Cultivate allies from day one. All the material I've ever seen on career success agree about this: Networking is vital to getting ahead. Make contacts from your very first day."[53]

While it may take extra initiative and extra effort for you to find and develop the critical contacts and relationships if you belong to a less-represented group, you can do it. And you must. It's the first

52. Ibid., p. 123.
53. Dudley, Denise M. *Every Woman's Guide to Career Success.* Mission, Kans.: SkillPath Publications, 1991, p. 39.

rule. Virtually everyone who succeeds professionally, regardless of category, does it that way.

Think of climbing the management ladder like playing a game of musical chairs in which it's legal to save seats. If you think everyone competes equally for the available seats, you're playing the wrong game. You need to find someone who will help save you a seat. That's the ultimate purpose of the mentoring process.

Types of Discriminatory Beliefs and Attitudes

It's interesting that most people whom you might consider racist or sexist don't think of themselves in those terms. Although the discriminatory effect may well be the same, there are a variety of different feelings and attitudes that produce discriminatory behavior. The reason you should understand the difference is that your coping response differs according to the reason for the discriminatory behavior.

Racism/sexism. An unambiguous racist or sexist believes it is a fact that for inherent (usually genetic) reasons, members of a given race, gender, or ethnicity are inferior. Those beliefs are normally hard to conceal, and come out in "classifying" statements that lump all members of the given group together. "All Blacks are. . . ." "All women are. . . ." "The thing about Latinos is. . . ."

There are two reasons why people with these beliefs argue— and actually believe—that they aren't actually racist or sexist. The first is that the expressed beliefs are not always correlated with an expression of hate. "Some of my best friends are Black/Jewish/ female!" comes the plaintive cry. "How can I be a racist/sexist/ prejudiced person?"

The second reason is these beliefs are often deeply held. "I'm not prejudiced; it's just a fact that Blacks/Jews/Latinos/women are. . . ." They may cite "proofs" of one sort or another to justify their beliefs.

It's not likely you'll be able to achieve much change in such a person's attitudes or belief structure. It's interesting, though, how often people with these attitudes make individual exceptions. "I believe what I believe about your group, but you're different. You're special."

In the practical world, if you are looking to move yourself into a power position where you achieve some change, the willingness of some people to grant exceptions may be something you can exploit or use as a means to an end. And perhaps if a person finds enough exceptions, he or she may end up questioning the inner assumption.

Misanthropy. Misogynists hate women; misanthropists hate humans in general. Angry and hateful people tend to lash out against others. Often, they have a kind of radar that lets them identify the most vulnerable places to attack others. For them, a racist or sexist remark is simply one more weapon on the rack, targeted to hurt its victim without regard for its intrinsic meaning. The issue is not whether the person actually believes what he or she is saying; the issue is whether it hurts, upsets, or humiliates you in a way that lets the attacker get his or her own way.

Psychologist Robert Bramson identifies the key observation about difficult people and their behavior: People behave in difficult ways because it works for them. It achieves their goals.[54]

Coping techniques, therefore, fall into two categories: helping them discover their techniques don't work on you, and helping them develop other ways of achieving their own goals. The overall strategy is assertiveness without combativeness, neutralizing the attack, and making it clear that you won't play the victim.

Class consciousness. Class-based discrimination can often be as pernicious and as damaging as racism or sexism, but it's often easier to deal with. For example, the stereotype that Black or Latino equals poor is fairly commonly held, and acts against all members of those groups regardless of the actual economic status of a given individual.

It's hard to overemphasize how much class consciousness drives the world of business, or how damaging class consciousness can be to those who are unaware of the game being played all around them. Paul Fussell writes, "We could gather as much from [*Dress for Success* author John T.] Molloy, whose talents are not at all contemptible, [who] designates himself 'America's first wardrobe engineer.' The ideal is for everyone in business to look upper-middle-class, because upper-middle-class equals Success. As he puts it with significant parallelism, 'Successful dress is really no more than achieving good taste and the look of the upper-middle class.' "[55]

54. Bramson, Robert M. *Coping With Difficult People.* New York: Doubleday/Anchor Press, 1981, p. 11.
55. Fussell, Paul. Op. cit., pp. 25–26.

Sound silly? Sound foolish? No doubt. But don't think for a minute it's not real.

The big advantage of classism over, say, racism or sexism, is that the signs of class membership can be simulated. In this case, the appearance *is* the reality.

Xenophobia. In an episode of the TV show *Murphy Brown,* a new broadcast executive overseeing the show turned out to be an African American. The humor in the episode focused on Murphy and her colleagues working ostentatiously to prove they were completely unaware of the race of their new manager, with the result that every word out of their mouths showed a painful, even embarrassing, degree of race consciousness.

Xenophobia is defined as "undue fear or contempt of strangers or foreigners, especially as reflected in political or cultural views." Literally meaning fear of strangers, this common fear often produces racist or sexist behavior as a consequence. People may mean well, but have difficulty opening dialogue, or they may let their xenophobia shade into anger, resentment, and racism.

In practice, something is strange and foreign to the extent we're not familiar with it. We find it inherently discomfiting to be around people whom we perceive as different from us. In a society where racial and cultural segregation is common, we have relatively little opportunity to meet people outside our own groups.

The general skill of putting people at ease is valuable across the board; it's particularly valuable when xenophobia is present. While it may well be true that you are as uncomfortable as anyone else, it's unfortunate but true that it has always been the new person who carries the burden of ice breaking.

Of course, while we may be strange and foreign to those around us in some ways, we are at least potentially familiar and comfortable in others. The two basic strategies, then, are (1) to open the door to air areas of potential sensitivity, and (2) to identify areas of common interest to serve as a foundation for relationship building.

What to Do When Coping Techniques Don't Work

In many situations, ordinary coping techniques will at least reduce the problem to manageable proportions. While it may not be possible to make the situation go away completely, you may be able to solve some of it and tolerate the rest.

What happens when you can't? You may need to take action.

Your internal organizational policies—and the law—mandate

remedies for discriminatory behavior practiced against protected groups. The problem is that all too often you end up with a Pyrrhic victory—you have to pay too heavy a price for your own victory.

Fortunately, the steps you must take to provide a foundation for potential legal action are the same steps you would take to achieve a more peaceful resolution.

Work journal. Mike Duncan recommends keeping a work journal. He says, "There are three primary reasons for a journal. First, it is the best systematic way to measure the progress of your own development. Second, keeping a journal is the best way to give yourself constant positive feedback. Third, the use of your journal becomes a way of thinking problems through, resolving them, and in the process, learning how to become more effective at problem solving."[56]

An important fourth reason we would add is to expand your journal to keep a private, objective record of the events of your workplace. An isolated incident of sexist or racist behavior, even if egregious, is often insufficient to demonstrate real discrimination. It is more often a pattern of events that take place over time. If you keep a work journal that is objective, timely, and accurate, you'll be able to look at it to identify patterns or problems that may exist.

Informal processes. You must normally pursue informal and internal methods to redress any grievances you have before you can pursue a more formal case. Ideally, you can resolve your problems informally so you don't need to move forward. Even if you feel the effort is destined to prove futile, you need to take those initial steps as well and as thoroughly as you possibly can, for two reasons. First, you might be wrong, and the process might actually work. Second, the credibility your complaint will have in the formal process is significantly affected by your showing that you did your best to resolve it unofficially.

If information in your journal has the potential for causing a problem, keep the journal at home and write in it each night. Remember to put facts and descriptions, not judgments, opinions, or evaluations, on the paper. Imagine that everything you write will be read aloud in a court that is not sympathetic to you. It probably won't, but it's a good idea to prepare for the worst eventuality.

Allies. Use the network of allies and mentors you build up to apply leverage on your behalf. That's what "old boys" do to resolve

56. Duncan, Mike. Op. cit., p. 19.

their problems; that's still the most powerful technique available to you.

Don't expect others to be able to solve your problem for you. Robert Bramson observes, ''The reality [that you're unlikely to be rescued] is a particularly bitter pill for those who have loyally supported and served their organizations. But unfair or not, fellow employees [and managers] are unlikely to do much to ease your pain, at least until you have first made some serious efforts at coping.''[57]

Allies are useful—indeed, they are essential—but they are also insufficient. Use all of the tools available to you.

COPING WITH DISCRIMINATION

1. What specific disadvantages do I perceive I am experiencing because of my race, gender, ethnicity, or religion?

    _____

    _____

    _____

2. To what extent, if any, do others not part of my group suffer the same or similar incidents?

    _____

    _____

    _____

3. How can I objectively document any patterns of behavior I perceive?

    _____

    _____

    _____

---

57. Bramson, Robert M. *Coping With Difficult Bosses*. New York: Simon & Schuster/Fireside Books, 1992, p. 5.

4. What internal, informal, and private steps can I take to counteract or counterbalance the negative impact?

    _____

    _____

    _____

5. What allies are available to me? How can I expand my network of allies and supporters?

    _____

    _____

    _____

6. What other resources do I have that will enable me to solve my problem?

    _____

    _____

    _____

7. Mixed in with the discriminatory behavior, are there any valid issues or concerns that have been raised about my job performance that I need to address?

    _____

    _____

    _____

Chapter 59

Learn How to Deal With Problem Bosses

A few bosses fit in the world-class bad boss category. Those walking nightmares are the extreme, and fortunately are quite rare. Sometimes the only solution is to go somewhere else. Most of the time, however, you can not only cope but actually prosper by learning to manage up.

The first step in the process of dealing with problem bosses is to verify that you are in fact taking the steps to increase your power and influence, build relationships, and demonstrate support that you've learned about in this book. Before you label someone "difficult," make sure you've thought about what you can do to influence his or her behavior and sometimes to modify your own.

Because of the inherent power differential between a boss and a subordinate, it's easy for you to feel powerless in the face of a problem boss. What are some of the things you can do specifically?

Understand Your Contribution to the Problem

First, always look at yourself and your possible contributions to the problem. This doesn't mean you're at fault, or even that you've done anything wrong at all. Nevertheless, you always have more power to change yourself and what you are doing than power to change others, and whenever that has an impact on other people, it's often the most powerful tool at your disposal to achieve change. Even if you haven't done anything wrong, you may not have done as much as you could that was right.

The topics discussed in this book are all part of how to manage up and prosper, regardless of the situation. They become even more important when applied to the specific challenges of managing a problem boss. Let's apply the major sections of this book to the problem boss situation:

- *Do good work.* If the quality of your work can be challenged, notice that your leverage is strongly reduced with your boss, and your ability to appeal for help at higher levels in the organization is also lessened.

  Whenever you are in a conflict with your boss that has a chance of getting ugly or spreading, or becoming formal in any way, take a hard look at yourself and your own flaws, even if they are minor compared to what is being done unfairly to you. You can expect that the defense of your boss (and your organization, if it comes to that) will be that you were incompetent or deficient yourself. The more you correct any potential problems, the better your situation will be.

- *Observe your boss's style.* If yours is primarily a style conflict (Focuser/Relater or Integrator/Operator), then make the style adjustments yourself to improve your coping ability. It's your job to adjust to your boss more than it is your boss's job to adjust to you.

- *Figure out your boss's likes and dislikes.* Do you have a problem boss, or just a normal boss with some pet peeves and annoying characteristics? Identify what part of the behavior you can live with, realizing that no one is perfect, and what parts of the behavior must change.

  The Pareto Principle says that one must separate the vital few from the trivial many. The best job in the world will be about 80 percent rewarding and positive and 20 percent dumpy and unpleasant. Into every life some rain must fall, and it's important to establish what you can live with.

- *Make sure you're in tune with your boss's goals.* If your boss perceives that your goals are in conflict with his or her own, a bad relationship is almost inevitable. Find as many points of mutual interest as you can, and build on those. Make sure you demonstrate through your behavior that you are supportive of those goals, especially in cases in which you interact with other departments and other managers. Relationships outside your department contain the possibility of threat and anxiety.

- *Learn how to negotiate like a pro.* When working with a highly aggressive boss, your negotiation skills become critical to your survival. Use ideas of win/win negotiation and your own clear vision to improve your strength in the relationship. You'll find that mutual respect is likely to result.

  Remember that the key issue in win/win negotiation has to do with your ability to see the situation as the other person sees it. That's the essential political skill, and one worth your time and effort to develop.

- *Give negative feedback well.* If your boss is driving you crazy and you haven't ever told him or her what the problem behavior is, don't expect any change. If you've told him or her and haven't gotten the desired change, use the Negative Feedback Model to improve your approach. Remember that it may take several rounds of negative feedback properly delivered to achieve the desired change.

- *Prepare for your meetings.* If the problem behavior centers around meetings or comes out in meetings (shouting, droning on and on, conflict or decision avoidance, etc.), prepare both content and strategic approaches to reduce the problem.

  Content involves making meetings more substantial in terms of agenda items, setting goals for meetings, and applying techniques for improving your meeting management. Strategic approaches include techniques such as trying to expand the meeting group to include others from outside your boss's command hierarchy who can give feedback or take action you cannot.

- *Give credit and praise generously.* One of the most powerful tools ever discovered to change behavior is the power of positive reinforcement. Most problem bosses don't behave badly 100 percent of the time. Identify good behavior and reinforce it regularly. Remember that this strategy takes time to be fully effective. Give credit if you suspect that paranoia or poor self-esteem are at work.

- *Build mentoring and networking relationships throughout the organization.* Although using your relationships to undercut the problem boss may seem like an attractive strategy, it's fraught with danger. Even if the strategy succeeds in damaging the problem boss, it will still come back to haunt you. Getting coping advice and support, making sure the problem boss doesn't darken your name, and understanding the wider context of the problem may give you some important tools to achieve change.

- *Demonstrate total loyalty and respect the chain of command.* This may be difficult advice to follow in dealing with a problem boss, but if you plan to stay in the organization, it's critical. Don't assume that your boss's bad behavior goes unnoticed by senior management. Depending on your boss's overall performance, a certain amount of bad behavior may be tolerated. Build your own independent relationships but make sure you stay completely supportive. Many problem bosses are dealing with their own insecurity and fear, which motivates the problem behavior. Any behavior on your part that could be labeled "disloyal" is likely to provoke more of what you don't want, not less.

- *Limit the "great ideas" and sell them effectively.* We've learned one of the key issues for our boss is to have as few headaches as possible. The bigger the problem with your boss, the more you should focus—for now—on getting the job done smoothly. Only rock the boat when you have access to the oars.

- *Be aware of what's going on, but don't get "political."* Being perceived as political in the negative sense is about the worst thing that can happen to you in dealing with a problem boss. You'll be perceived as trying to undercut and destroy the boss, whether or not that's your intent. Practice the "Four R's" of building your political power in an ethical way, and some of that power may help you successfully deal with the problem boss.

- *Work on better communication.* Make sure you're saying no in the right way, whether it involves overloading job assignments or inappropriate tasks. Ensure that you have the documentation and support you need to justify those nos. Consider keeping a work log and providing a "5-15" Report or other regular reports on your work activities and issues to help keep your boss informed.

- *Build your skills and knowledge in management.* Especially if there are areas in which you have trouble because your boss is knowledgeable and you are ignorant, focus on developing the skills and knowledge to be part of the dialogue. For example, if you don't know anything about finance, you must accept anything your boss says about the subject. If there are areas in which your boss thinks he or she is knowledgeable but is really not, work at helping your boss acquire better knowledge; it will only help you.

- *Arrange for your own performance appraisals on a regular basis.* When criticism of you is general in nature, it's almost impossible for you to do anything constructive or appropriate about it. This is called the "bring me a rock problem," and it works like this:

Your boss says, "Bring me a rock." You reply, "What kind of rock?" The boss says, "A rock, stupid!"

You go get a rock, and the boss says, "That's not the rock I wanted." You say, "Well, what kind of rock do you want?" The boss replies, "A rock! How much clearer can I get? All I want is a simple rock, and you can't even do that!"

You get another rock, and are greeted with disgust and disdain. "That's not right, either. Do I have to do everything myself around here?" And the pattern goes on.

When faced with "bring me a rock," you need to get a definition, but your boss doesn't want to give you a definition, because then your success or failure is dependent on your boss's whim at any given moment. You need to build a foundation of definition in order to have any hope of dealing with this dilemma.

The basic strategy is to try to achieve agreement on mutual expectations before you get specific assignments. By approaching your boss about negotiating a performance expectations list, you begin to identify the specifics that move you out of that box.

What if you're not successful? A second technique is to begin confirming all assignments in writing and set your own expectations of the job as you understand it. This also runs some risk, depending on how much the boss wants to keep you off balance. If that technique fails, keep your own work diary and log of what you've done. Consider writing a "5-15" Report each week. If the alleged failure to meet expectations shows up on your performance appraisal, you need objective documentation to overcome your boss's opinion. At the very least, your boss will want to think twice about what goes on a piece of paper.

- *Find the hidden keys to the executive suite.* The keys to the executive suite can be rational or irrational. Either way, you must know what the keys are.

One key that is always a consideration is that your boss's opposition to your advancement is an extreme—possibly even fatal—negative, whether your boss has reasonable or irrational and petty reasons to oppose you. And, it's almost always a mistake to tackle it directly, because an attack on one manager, even if justified, is normally taken as an attack on management in general. We all have a basic tendency to "circle the wagons" when a member of our group is attacked from outside the group, even if on some level we agree with the criticisms being leveled. When employees attack managers, all management feels threatened.

It may be in your best interest to pursue a lateral move rather than try for career advancement. If you approach other managers instead of your boss to solicit their help in your career move, downplay or ignore any conflicts with your boss, and instead focus on broadening your operational experience and background to fit you for later promotion.

A woman applied for a movie critic job at a large regional newspaper; she had extensive background and qualifications for the job. The reason given for not hiring her was, "You don't know how to cover a fire." In other words, all members of the journalism staff, regardless of actual experience, needed to be general assignment reporters at heart.

In many organizations, for example, someone from a staff department may simply not be a candidate for more senior roles, because everyone who is executive material has a background in (choose one) operations, sales and marketing, finance, etc. The right lateral move can often do more for your career than a promotion on a dead-end ladder.

- *Develop a personal intelligence network in your organization.* "If caught or killed," the opening of *Mission Impossible* goes, "the secretary will disavow any knowledge of your activities."

One of the dangers you face in building an intelligence network is getting caught at it, usually a sign of either being too obvious or crossing the line from legitimate intelligence-gathering activities into shadier activities. You can also get into trouble simply for "knowing too much" if that knowledge starts to make your boss suspicious.

Remember that bosses themselves can be politically isolated within the organization, have enemies of their own, and be left out of critical information. This leads to a tendency to be suspicious, resentful, and even paranoid about any member of their work group reaching out within the organization and gathering her or his own information. "Just because you're paranoid," the saying goes, "doesn't mean people aren't out to get you," and if your boss has powerful enemies—or believes he or she has—the problems can rebound on you.

The fundamental technique is to make sure you use your information to advance your boss's goals—to be useful and informative and supportive without waiting to be asked. Only to the extent that your intelligence network benefits your boss will your boss be able to be reasonably comfortable with it. The nice side benefit is that at the same time your boss profits from your intelligence network, your boss will necessarily have to provide you some respect and slack, on the grounds that you have the power to revoke or change the use of the information. Don't ever suggest that; it will only turn your boss into an implacable enemy because we hate most what we fear. Be assured that your boss will figure it out and hope that you do not.

- *Learn how to delegate.* In a world in which we are asked to do more and more with less and less, your ability to get others to cooperate, support, and help you achieve your objectives is a critical career skill.

  Remember that part of managing your delegation environment is knowing when to accept, when to reject, and when to negotiate delegations given to you.

- *Build connections with other departments.* The key caution here is to be aware of your boss's personal relationships with those other departments and any historical rivalry or enmity between the departments.

  In one organization, there was significant bad blood between the product development group and the legal department over the application of trademark laws. One person who tried to build connections and relationships with the legal department found himself frozen out of any discussions or strategies in his own work group because of suspicions of disloyalty. People were being forced to take sides, and he was not considered for certain advancement opportunities because he wasn't being a "team player."

  Was he really disloyal? No, but that hardly mattered. The perception was the problem. What he could have done differently was: first, to be aware of the conflict and how it would affect others' perceptions of him; second, to use the influence and information to support the agenda of his own boss; third, to try to build bridges toward problem solving and improved relationships.

  In a war, it's hard to stay neutral.

- *Deal effectively with stereotypes and prejudices.* The law ostensibly protects you in cases of discrimination based on gender, race, ethnicity, religion, and, in some states, sexual orientation. However, if you have to resort to the law to protect yourself, you lose—at least, you suffer along with whatever suffering you can force on the organization or individuals who have discriminated against you. A lawsuit takes time, contains risk, invites retaliation (including efforts to discredit you by finding and emphasizing any ways in which your own performance has been less than perfect), and causes other employers to view you with suspicion (if they know what has happened—remember the "circle the wagons" tendency).

There are times and situations when that's the best you can do. There are times in which it is right and necessary to sacrifice yourself for the good of others who will follow in your footsteps. But never forget there's a price. If you can solve the situation short of formal action, that's frequently best for you, as well as others who may be concerned.

In addition, when you seek formal action, you must always be able to demonstrate that you've worked within the informal resolution process, and you need to take a hard look at yourself to see if you have any areas vulnerable to counterattack. It doesn't matter if they did most of the wrong; if you did part, expect that to be prominently featured.

Diagnose the Situation

You can also use more specific ideas for managing problem bosses.

Virtually any bad or problem behavior is the result of numerous influences and factors. While a direct assault on the core problem may be appropriate, sometimes you can improve your leverage elsewhere. "Difficult people" expert Paul Friedman observes that "each person and procedure is an element in a *system* [emphasis added], and each affects the others. Change in any one element will change what is occurring in the system."[58]

For example, let's imagine that your boss practices conflict avoidance. Why is the person behaving that way? Let's look at some common possibilities:

- Dislike of strong emotion
- Fear of higher authority
- Desire not to be disliked
- Fear of taking personal responsibility
- Belief that others dislike being told what to do

The behavior can be the result of any one or a combination of those reasons. Through observation, knowing the person, or experimentation, you might be able to determine what some of the underlying ideas might be. If the issue is dislike of strong emotion, make sure your emotions are calm and reassuring. If the issue is fear of

58. Friedman, Paul G. *How to Deal With Difficult People*. Mission, Kans.: SkillPath Publications, 1991, p. 12.

higher authority, provide supporting documentation, information, and any networking influence you have to reduce any risks for your boss.

Select and Use a Communications Strategy

Whether you use the Negative Feedback Model, a negotiation strategy, or simply modify your style in managing your problem boss, it's important to communicate about the problem if you are to have any hope of change.

Because of the emotional stress involved in the situation, you should prepare before having the communication. Don't try to "wing it." Make notes, identify likely responses, and list your key points.

Make a Plan

Ideally, you can negotiate a mutual plan with the problem boss to achieve the desired change. Sometimes the strategy is to make your own plan based on your knowledge and the events that have occurred, and implement it on your own. A plan can involve different communications and behaviors you will do, reactions you will take based on your boss's behavior, or long-range plans to change your situation.

Decide What to Do If the Plan Doesn't Work

Don't give up on a plan too quickly. People don't become problem bosses overnight, and they won't unlearn overnight either. It's still a good idea to decide what you will do in the event that you can't get the necessary change accomplished. Is the situation so bad you'll have to leave the organization, or is it a tolerable annoyance? Can you get a transfer or reassignment? Can you change elements of your work situation so you don't confront the problem behavior quite as often? Whatever you decide, follow through.

COPING WITH PROBLEM BOSSES
FIVE-POINT PLAN

1. Diagnose the situation in behavioral terms.

    _____

    _____

    _____

2.   Identify your contributions to the situation.

_____

_____

_____

3.   Develop and implement a communications strategy.

_____

_____

_____

4.   Make a plan.

_____

_____

_____

5.   Decide what to do if the plan doesn't work.

_____

_____

_____

Conclusion

You've learned many different ways to manage up, and you've also learned that the most effective ways to improve your relationship with your boss are also the most effective ways to deliver good staff support, do a great job, and be a team player. That's not a coincidence. The goal of this book was never to show you how to be a better manipulator, but rather to be the sort of effective professional whose influence is great because it is truly earned.

You've also realized that some of these tips are more valuable to you right now than others, both because each situation is unique and because you already have some of the skills and aptitudes cited in these pages.

Now it's time to go to work. Pick the most essential and valuable places to start and set your action plan. Start small and build from there. Remember the cautions you learned in the introduction:

- Make the affirmative decision that you will go first.
- Don't expect overnight miracles.
- Practice consistency in your efforts.
- Understand that it's always a two-way street, but the power dynamic between you and your boss isn't equal and never will be.
- Look around at other employee-boss relationships.
- Start slow.
- Start today.

And before you know it, you'll find yourself MANAGING UP!

Bibliography and Suggested Reading

Alessandra, Tony. *Mastering Your Message.* Audiotape. Mission, Kans.: SkillPath Publications, 1997.

Andersen, Richard, and Helene Hinis. *Write It Right: A Guide for Clear and Correct Writing.* Mission, Kans.: SkillPath Publications, 1993.

Bapes, Robert P. E-mail to author, 20 February 1999.

Bemis, Warren, and Burt Nanus. *Leaders: The Strategies for Taking Charge.* New York: HarperPerennial, 1985.

Block, Peter. *The Empowered Manager: Positive Political Skills at Work.* San Francisco: Jossey-Bass, 1987.

Bramson, Robert M. *Coping With Difficult Bosses.* New York: Simon & Schuster/Fireside Books, 1992.

Bramson, Robert M. *Coping With Difficult People.* New York: Doubleday/Anchor Press, 1981.

Brown, Jerry, and Denise Dudley. *The Supervisor's Guide.* Mission, Kans.: SkillPath Publications, 1989.

Burley-Allen, Madelyn. *Managing Assertively: How to Improve Your People Skills.* New York: John Wiley & Sons, 1983.

Canfield, Jack. *How to Build High Self-Esteem.* Audiotape. Chicago: Nightingale-Conant, 1989.

Canfield, Jack, and Mark Victor Hansen, eds. *Chicken Soup for the Soul.* Deerfield Beach, Fla.: Health Communications, 1993.

Caro, Robert A. *The Power Broker: Robert Moses and the Fall of New York*. New York: Alfred A. Knopf, 1974.

Caroselli, Marlene. *Meetings That Work*. Mission, Kans.: SkillPath Publications, 1992.

Carr-Ruffino, Norma. *The Promotable Woman*. 2d ed. Belmont, Calif.: Wadsworth, 1993.

Clark, Ann D., and Patt Perkins. *Surviving Your Boss: How to Cope With Office Politics and Get on With Your Job*. New York: Citadel Press, 1996.

Clarke, Colleen. *Networking: How to Creatively Tap Your People Resources*. Mission, Kans.: SkillPath Publications, 1993.

Contini, Lisa. *Assert Yourself!* Mission, Kans.: SkillPath Publications, 1996.

Danis, Julie. "It's a Living: Networking by Any Other Name Is Just Part of Life." *Chicago Tribune*, 28 February 1999, Section 6, p. 1.

Dauten, Dale. "Corporate Curmudgeon: Time Expansion—A Window to Creativity." *Chicago Tribune*, 21 February 1999, Section 5, p. 8.

Davies, Dave. *Letters and Memos Just Like That!* Mission, Kans.: SkillPath Publications, 1997.

Dawson, Roger. *The Secrets of Power Negotiating*. Audiotape. Chicago: Nightingale-Conant, 1987.

Dobson, Michael. *Exploring Personality Styles*. Mission, Kans.: SkillPath Publications, 1999.

Dobson, Michael. *The Juggler's Guide to Managing Multiple Projects*. Sylva, N.C.: Project Management Institute, 1999.

Dobson, Michael. *Practical Project Management*. Mission, Kans.: SkillPath Publications, 1996.

Dobson, Michael Singer, and Deborah Singer Dobson. *Coping With Supervisory Nightmares*. Mission, Kans.: SkillPath Publications, 1997.

DuBrin, Andrew. *Winning Office Politics: DuBrin's Guide for the '90s*. New York: Prentice Hall, 1990.

Dudley, Denise M. *Every Woman's Guide to Career Success*. Mission, Kans.: SkillPath Publications, 1991.

Duncan, Mike. *Reach Your Goals in Spite of the Old Boy Network: A Guide for African American Employees.* Edgewood, Md.: Duncan & Duncan, 1990.

England, Dan. *Welcome to the "Real" Corporate World: Surviving and Succeeding in a Large Corporation.* Greenfield Center, N.Y.: Greenfield Center Press, 1994.

Fielder, Barbara. *Motivation in the Workplace.* Mission, Kans.: SkillPath Publications, 1996.

Finkler, Steven A. *The Complete Guide to Finance & Accounting for Nonfinancial Managers.* Englewood Cliffs, N.J.: Prentice Hall, 1983.

Fisher, Roger. *Beyond Machiavelli: Tools for Coping With Conflict.* New York: Penguin Books, 1996.

Fisher, Roger, and William Ury. *Getting to Yes: Negotiating Agreement Without Giving In.* New York: Penguin Books, 1981.

Frame, J. Davidson. *Managing Projects in Organizations: How to Make the Best Use of Time, Techniques, and People, rev. ed.* San Francisco: Jossey-Bass, 1995, pp. 28–31.

Friedman, Paul G. *How to Deal With Difficult People.* Mission, Kans.: SkillPath Publications, 1991.

Fuller, George. *The First-Time Supervisor's Survival Guide.* Englewood Cliffs, N.J.: Prentice Hall, 1995.

Fussell, Paul. *Class.* New York: Ballantine Books, 1983.

Goleman, Daniel. *Emotional Intelligence.* New York: Bantam Books, 1995.

Grotjahn, Martin. *Beyond Laughter: Humor and the Subconscious.* New York: McGraw-Hill, 1970.

Grout, Pam. *The Mentoring Advantage.* Mission, Kans.: SkillPath Publications, 1995.

Gunlicks, L. F. *The Machiavellian Manager's Handbook for Success.* Washington, D.C.: Libey Publishing/Regnery, 1993.

Gustafson, Dave. E-mail to author, 21 February 1999.

Haley, Ivy. *Discovering Your Purpose.* Mission, Kans.: SkillPath Publications, 1996.

Hartley, Robert F. *Marketing Mistakes*. 3d ed. New York: John Wiley & Sons, 1986.

Hathaway, Patti, and Susan D. Schubert. *Managing Upward: Strategies for Succeeding With Your Boss*. Los Altos, Calif.: Crisp Publications, 1992.

Heinlein, Robert A. *Double Star*. New York: Signet/New American Library, 1957.

Hendrickson, Robert. *QPB Encyclopedia of Word and Phrase Origins*. New York: Facts on File, 1997.

Hoff, Ron. *I Can See You Naked. rev. ed.* Kansas City, Mo.: Andrews and McMeel, 1992.

Imai, Masaaki. *Kaizen: The Key to Japan's Competitive Success*. New York: McGraw-Hill, 1986.

Jablonski, Joseph. *Implementing Total Quality Management: An Overview*. San Diego, Calif.: Pfeiffer & Co., 1991.

Jandt, Fred C. *Straight Answers to People Problems*. Burr Ridge, Ill.: Irwin Professional Publishing, 1994.

Kaltman, Al. *Cigars, Whiskey, and Winning: Leadership Lessons From General Ulysses S. Grant*. New York: Prentice Hall, 1998.

Kaye, Harvey. *Decision Power: How to Make Successful Decisions With Confidence*. Englewood Cliffs, N.J.: Prentice Hall, 1992.

Kaye, Zoie. *Saying "No" to Negativity: How to Manage Negativity in Yourself, Your Boss, and Your Co-Workers*. Mission, Kans.: SkillPath Publications, 1996.

Kennedy, Marilyn Moats. *Office Politics*. Audiotape. Chicago: Nightingale-Conant, 1989.

Korda, Michael. "Power: How to Get It, How to Use It." in *What the Pros Say About Success*. Audiotape. New York: American Management Association/Simon & Schuster Audio Division, 1986.

Kramer, Robert. E-mail to author, 19 February 1999.

Lantz, Roy. *The Care and Keeping of Customers*. Mission, Kans.: SkillPath Publications, 1995.

Laufer, Alexander. *Simultaneous Management: Managing Projects in a Dynamic Environment*. New York: AMACOM, 1997.

Lee, Stan, and Steve Ditko. "Spider-Man!" *Amazing Fantasy*. Issue 15, August 1962.

Lewis, H. W. *Why Flip a Coin? The Art and Science of Good Decisions*. New York: John Wiley & Sons, 1997.

McGraw, Nanci. *Organized for Success! 95 Tips for Taking Control of Your Time, Your Space, and Your Life*. Mission, Kans.: SkillPath Publications, 1995.

McGraw, Robert. *Learning to Laugh at Work*. Mission, Kans.: SkillPath Publications, 1995.

McKay, Harvey. *Dig Your Well Before You're Thirsty: The Only Networking Book You'll Ever Need*. New York: Currency/Doubleday, 1997.

O'Neill, Tip, with Gary Hymel. *All Politics Is Local: And Other Rules of the Game*. New York: Times Books/Random House, 1994.

Pachter, Barbara, and Marjorie Brody. *Climbing the Corporate Ladder: What You Need to Know and Do to Be a Promotable Person*. Mission, Kans.: SkillPath Publications, 1995.

Peters, Tom, and Brian Tracy. *Management Advantage*. Audiotape. Chicago: Nightingale-Conant, 1989.

Poley, Michelle Fairfield. *Mastering the Art of Communication: Your Keys to Developing a More Effective Personal Style*. Mission, Kans.: SkillPath Publications, 1995.

Pope, Alexander. "An Essay on Criticism" line 362, in Tillotson, Geoffrey, Paul Fussell, Jr., and Marshall Waingrow. *Eighteenth Century Literature*. New York: Harcourt, Brace & World, 1969.

Pryor, Fred. *Ask Fred Pryor About Working With People*. Shawnee Mission, Kans.: Pryor Resources, 1987.

Rosenberg, Arthur D., and Ellen Fuchs Thorn. *Manipulative Memos: Control Your Career Through the Medium of the Memo*. Berkeley, Calif.: Ten Speed Press, 1994.

Salmon, William A., and Rosemary T. Salmon. *Office Politics for the Utterly Confused*. New York: McGraw-Hill, 1999.

Schroeder, Ruth, and Joel Schroeder. *Putting Anger to Work for You!* Mission, Kans.: SkillPath Publications, 1995.

Shaw, George Bernard. "Pygmalion." in Stanley Weintraub, ed. *The Portable Bernard Shaw*. New York: Viking Portable Library, 1977.

Silver, Susan. *Organized to Be the Best! New Timesaving Ways to Simplify and Improve How You Work*. Los Angeles: Adams-Hall Publishing, 1991.

Tannen, Deborah. *Talking From 9 to 5: How Women's and Men's Conversational Styles Affect Who Gets Heard, Who Gets Credit, and What Gets Done at Work*. New York: William Morrow, 1994.

Temme, Jim. *Productivity Power*. Mission, Kans.: SkillPath Publications, 1993.

Walton, Mary. *The Deming Management Method*. New York: Perigee, 1986.

Wilson, Robert Anton. *The Illuminati Papers*. Berkeley, Calif.: Ronin Publishing, 1990.

Ziglar, Zig. *Goals*. Audiotape. Chicago: Nightingale-Conant, 1988.

Ziglar, Zig. "How to Get What You Want." *What the Pros Say About Success*. Audiotape. New York: American Management Association/Simon & Schuster Audio Division, 1978.

About the Authors

MICHAEL SINGER DOBSON is an author, consultant, and popular seminar leader in project management, communications, and personal success who brings a unique practical perspective to what works in the real world. He has trained people in well over 1,000 organizations on three continents on topics ranging from project management to career strategies. His down-to-earth style and practical advice come from his management career positions, including vice president of Discovery Software, Inc.; vice president/marketing & sales of Games Workshop, Inc.; and director of marketing and product development for TSR, Inc. He was a member of the research team that created and opened the Smithsonian National Air and Space Museum, the world's most popular museum. He is the author of *Practical Project Management* and *The Juggler's Guide to Managing Multiple Projects*.

DEBORAH SINGER DOBSON, M.Ed., is vice president for human resources for GATX Terminals Corporation in Chicago, and was cofounder and executive director of ERIS Enterprises, Inc., a twelve-person management consulting firm based in Maryland. An expert in organizational development and management effectiveness, she has consulted for numerous Fortune 500 companies in the areas of quality, team building, leadership, and cultural diversity, and has lectured on the topic of training return on investment strategies.

The Dobsons have coauthored the book/video/audio series *Coping With Supervisory Nightmares*, and the video and audio program *Training Skills for Team Leaders*. They live in the Chicago suburbs with their son Jamie and two Shelties.

Index

abusive behavior, 102
accessories, fashion, 78
accomplishment, as power, 125
accounting, 144–145
active listening, 99
advance warnings, 18–19
African Americans, 214, 215
agenda(s)
    hidden, 199–201
    for visits to boss, 55
Alcoholics Anonymous, 48
allies
    boss's, 208–210
    creating network of, 219–220
Allstate Insurance Company, 173
anger, appropriate use of, 49
appearances, 126
appraisals, *see* performance ap-
    praisals
Ask-Observe-Experiment process, 4,
    36–37
assertiveness, 86–89, 137
    and abusive behavior, 102
    consequences of, 87
    and fighting, 49
    as goal, 62
    in negotiation, 46
    in nonverbal communication,
    87–88
    planning for, 86–87
    as power, 125

and praise, 83
    self-assessment of, 89
assessment(s)
    of ability to handle criticism, 110
    of ability to sell ideas, 117
    of assertiveness, 89
    of assistance to boss, 40
    of bad moods, 103
    of "big picture," 119–120
    of boss's allies/enemies, 210
    of boss's likes/dislikes, 27
    of boss's times of day, 29
    of communication effectiveness,
    137
    of decision-making skills, 130
    of discrimination, 220–221
    of fighting, 53–54
    of 5-15 Report, 160–161
    of goals, 37–38
    of "goodmouthing," 42
    of "good work," 5–6
    of hidden agendas, 201
    of influence skills, 198
    of informativeness, 93
    of involvement with trade/pro-
    fessional organizations, 12
    of job assignments, 188
    of listening, 100
    of management "monkeys," 185
    of meeting effectiveness, 71
    of mentoring/networking, 98

assessment(s) *(continued)*
  of paperwork, 32
  of personal honesty, 22
  of personal organization, 112
  of problem handling, 19
  of professional image, 78–79
  of promotion plans, 212–213
  of relationships, 75–76
  of relationship with boss, 122–
    123, 132
  of responsibility, 66
  of sense of humor, 141–142
  of status symbols, 174
  of threats, 63–64
  of time management, 139
  of training skills, 151
  of trust/loyalty, 108
  of working with others, 8–9
  of work performance, 164
  of writing skills, 149
assignments, going after important,
    186–188
associations, professional, 10–11
authority, 72–73

background tests, 166–167
"bad days," 28
bad moods, 101–103
"badmouthing," 41
Bapes, Bob, 160
BATNA, 45
behavioral language, 58
"big picture," 118–120, 126
blame
  taking, 65, 129
  unfair, 92
Blanchard, Ken, 81
body language, 88
boss(es)
  background of, 121–122
  bad mood in, 101
  comparisons with, 63

  as customer, 131–132
  desire of, to be managed, 104–105
  energy cycle of, 28–29
  "face time" with, 55
  and fighting, 50–51
  function of, xii
  goals of, 37, 223–224, 227–228
  helping with success of, 39–40
  identifying allies/enemies of,
    208–210
  likes/dislikes of, 23–27
  as meeting leader/participant, 70
  and mentors, 95
  and paperwork, 30–32
  power of, xi
  "problem," xiii–xiv
  qualifications of, xiii
  recognizing humanity of, 121–123
  self-directed, 25
  style of, 4, 13–17, 223
  visits to, 55–56
  weak points of, xiii
brainstorming, 21–22
Bramson, Robert
  on difficult people, 217
  on expecting others to solve prob-
    lems, 220
Broadcast News (film), 96
brown nosing, 83, 95
Bryant, Paul "Bear," on credit and
    blame, 65
Burley-Allen, Madelyn, on handling
    criticism, 109

Canfield, Jack, on Victory Log, 110
Career Limiting Move (CLM), 114
Caro, Robert, 209
Carr-Ruffino, Norma
  on listening, 99
  on loyalty, 105
Casual Friday, 78
Celine's Second Law, 136

Central Intelligence Agency (CIA), 177
chain of command, 106–107, 225
chain-of-command issues, 92
change, as goal of communication, 31
charitable activities, 11
"check-ins," 4
CIA (Central Intelligence Agency), 177
clarity
   in communication, 133, 135
   in negotiation, 46
classism, 217–218
CLM (Career Limiting Move), 114
closed-ended promises, 21
closed-ended questions, 59
clothing, 77–78
cognitive dissonance, 36
colleagues, 7, 192
common interests, 168
communication(s)
   assertiveness in, 87–88
   effectiveness in, 58
   goal of, 31
   in hierarchies, 136–137
   at meetings, 69
   nonverbal, 87–88, 136
   as power, 126
   with problem bosses, 225
   as skill, 133–137
   strategy for, 230
   verbal vs. paper, 30
   see also listening
comparisons, 63
competition
   for resources, 209
   in workplace, 7–8
compliments
   accepting, 41
   phony, 83
compromise, 53

conflicts
   with boss's vision, 153
   between departments, 209
   resolution of, 51–53
   and threats, 62
coping techniques, 217–219
corporate culture
   and documentation, 31
   and personal relationships, 74–75
Cover Your Assets (CYA), 31
credential tests, 166–167
credibility, 116
credit
   giving, 224
   sharing, 65, 84
   taking, 129
criticism
   handling, 109–110
   negative feedback vs., 57
customer(s)
   boss as, 131–132
   treating other departments as, 205
customer service, 131
CYA (Cover Your Assets), 31

DBMP-BMA rule, 19
decision making, 129–130
   at meetings, 69
   styles of, 24
defensiveness, signs of, 88
delegation, 144, 183–184, 189–195, 228
Deming, W. Edwards, on slogans, 35
departments
   conflicts between, 209
   goals of, 36–37
   working with other, 202–207, 228
development, see professional development
"difficult people," 217
disagreements, 24
discipline, 73

discrimination, 214–221
  action steps for dealing with,
    218–220
  and barriers to advancement,
    215–216
  and lawsuits, 228–229
  types of, 216–218
disorganization, 111–112
documentation, 30–31, 125
dress, 77–79, 217
DuBrin, Andrew, on reason for
  being hired, 39
Dudley, Denise, on career success
  for women, 215
Dun & Bradstreet, 178
Duncan, Mike
  on African Americans and "old
    boy network," 214
  on work journals, 219

early, arriving, 163
e-mail, 30
emotional context, listening for,
  99–100
emotional impact of behavior, 59
Emotional Intelligence (Daniel
  Goleman), xii
endorphins, 141
enemies, boss's, 208–210
energy cycle, 28–29
enthusiasm, 35
"extra credit," 163
eye contact, 88

face-saving techniques
  and fighting, 49
  for negotiation, 46–47
"face time" with boss, 55
Farleyfile, 206
fashion accessories, 78
FEAR, 87

feedback
  asking for, 3–4
  negative, see negative feedback
  in performance appraisals, 154
  positive, 80–85
fence mending, 50
Fielder, Barbara, on ten-coin technique, 82–83
fighting, 48–54
  approach to, 50–51
  and boss, 50–51
  and conflict resolution, 51–53
  impersonal, 49
  principles of, 49–50
  self-assessment on, 53–54
finance, 144–145
Finkler, Steven, 144
The First-Time Supervisor's Survival
  Guide (George Fuller), 113
Fisher, Roger, on negotiation, 44
5-15 Report, 159–161
focusers, 14–16
Forbes, Malcolm, xiv
forms, 30–31
Friedman, Paul, on people in system, 229
friendly behavior, 73, 75
friendships, 73–74
Fuller, George, on impressing the
  boss, 113
fun, having, 74
Fussell, Paul, 217

"game films," 175
game theory, 130
Gantt Charts, 145
giving in to others, 51–52
goals
  and "big picture," 118
  of boss, 37, 223–224, 227–228
  departmental, 36–37
  fighting to achieve, 52–53

organizational, 8, 34–36
personal, 8, 34
for professional development, 5
setting, 33
types of, 33–34
Godzilla Principle, 18, 39
Goldberg, Rube, 81n.
Goleman, Daniel, xii
"goodmouthing," 41–42, 63
"good work," doing, 1–6
government information, 178–179
Grant, Ulysses S., 66
Grotjahn, Martin, 141
growth, xiii
Gunlicks, L. F., on colleagues, 7

Haley, Ivy, on career shaping, 34
"hard" negotiation, 44–45
Harvard Negotiation Project, 44
Heinlein, Robert A., on Farleyfiles, 206
Herbert, George, on good words, 41
Herzberg, Frederick, 81
hidden agendas, 199–201
hierarchical management structure, 106, 136–137
honesty, personal, 20–22
humor, 140–142

IBM, 74–75
ideas, "selling" your, 113–117
image, professional, 77–79
impressing the boss, 113–114
Incident Log, 175–176
independent project portfolios, 146
influence skills, 196–198
information
government, 178–179
press, 178
public, 178
trade/professional, 10
when to share, 90–92

information styles, 24–25
informative, being, 90–93
initiative, 212
as power, 125
tests of, 166
integrators, 14–16
intelligence network, personal, 177–181, 227
Internet, 178

job assignments, going after important, 186–188
job description, review of, 2
job performance, quality of, 1–6
jokes, 140
judgmental language, 58

Kaltman, Al, on lying, 22
keeping your word, 20
Kennedy, Marilyn Moats, 37, 72
K-I-S-S rule, 30
knowledge
as power, 125
trade/professional, 10
and training, 150
Korda, Michael, 173
Kramer, Bob, on "game films," 175

language
behavioral, 58
judgmental, 58
symbolic, 172–174
language styles, 25–26
Laufer, Alexander, on project surprises, 18–19
laughing, 141
"Law of the Slight Edge," 3
lawsuits, 228–229
leadership, and persuasion, xii
learning, lifelong, 5
Lewis, H. W., on quality of decisions, 129

lifelong learning, 5
line departments, 36n.
listening, 99–100, 136
   active, 99
   to mentor, 96
   and negative feedback, 59
   and negotiation, 46
   self-assessment of, 100
   to your own voice, 88
losing gracefully, 49–50
losing your temper, 49
loyalty, total, 105–106, 225
lying, 21, 22, 136

management
   definition of, xiv
   delegating to, 191
   dynamics of, xiii
   everyone's involvement in, xiv–xv
   function of, xii
   mutual, xiii
   project, 40, 145–146
   and responsibility, 65
   role of, in decisions, 25
   and supervision, 143–144
   time, 138–139
managers, managing, xiii
manipulation, 196–197
matrix management structure, 106
MBTI (Myers-Briggs Type Indica-
      tor), 14
McKay, Harvey, 162
meetings
   "bad," 28
   boss as leader/participant in, 70
   cost of bad, 67–69
   preparing for, 67–71
   with problem bosses, 224
   running good, 69–70
Memorandum for the Record, 31
memos, 30
mentoring, 94–96, 169–170, 224

misanthropy, 217
mission statements, 35–36
mistakes, 19
Molloy, John T., 217
"monkeys," 182–185
moods, bad, 101–103
more, doing, 162–164
motivating, 144
multiple projects, managing, 146
Murphy Brown, 218
mutual management, xiii
Myers-Briggs Type Indicator
      (MBTI), 14

Napoleon, on keeping one's word,
      21
negative feedback, 57–61
   and behavioral language, 58
   handling, 109–110
   with problem bosses, 224
   steps for giving, 58–60
Negative Feedback Model, 59–61,
      70, 110, 230
negotiation, 43–47
   and conflict resolution, 53
   of critical job elements, 153
   and decision-making style, 24
   "hard" vs. "soft" styles of, 44–45
   perceptions of, 43
   of performance appraisal, 155
   preparation worksheet for, 47
   principles of effective, 45–47
   with problem bosses, 224
   win/win, 8, 44, 53, 59
nervousness, signs of, 88
network, personal intelligence, 177–
      181, 227
networking, 10, 96–97, 224
neutral third parties, 46
no, saying, 20, 133–134, 138, 184–185
nonverbal communication, 87–88,
      136

objectives, performance, 2–3
office politics, 124–128, 225
   and appearances, 126
   and power, 125–126
   reality of, 124
   self-assessment of, 127–128
   tactics in, 124–125
"old boy network," 214, 219–220
O'Neill, Tip, 20, 208
open-ended promises, 21
open-ended questions, 59
operators, 14–16
organizational goals, 34–36
organized, getting, 111–112
Organized to Be the Best! (Susan Silver), 112
outsiders, delegating to, 194
overdelivering, 21

paper, handling, 112
paperwork, 30–32
paraphrasing, 46
Pareto Principle, 223
patience, in negotiation, 46
people skills, 126
performance, quality of, 1–6
performance appraisals, 152–158
   ideas for, 153–154
   lack of, 156
   meaningfulness of, 153
   negative, 154–155
   preparing for, 156–158
   with problem bosses, 225–226
performance objectives, 2–3
performance reviews, 4
performance standards, exceeding, 2–3
Performax DISC, 14
persistence, in negotiation, 46
personal goals, 34
personal honesty, 20–22

personal intelligence network, 177–181, 227
Personality Explorer, 14–17
personal relationships, 74
persuasion, xii
pet peeves, 26
plagiarism, 149
planning
   for assertiveness, 86–87
   setting aside time for, 138
politics, *see* office politics
Pope, Alexander, on ease in writing, 149
position power, limitations of, 202–203
positive feedback, 80–85
positive reinforcement, 81–82
power
   of boss, xi
   limitations of position, 202–203
   and office politics, 125–126
   and responsibility, 65
   walk-away, 45
praise, giving, 41, 80–85, 224
PRAISE model, 82–85
prejudice, *see* discrimination
press information, 178
priorities
   and "big picture," 118–120
   keeping track of, 40
   listening for, 100
prioritizing, 116
priority styles, 23–24
privacy, 46
"problem bosses," xiii–xiv, 222–231
problems, giving advance warning about, 18–19
procrastination, 139
productivity, 151
profession, getting involved in, 10–12
professional development, 5, 153

professional image, 77–79
professional relationships, 73
project management, 40, 145–146
promises, making, 20–21
promotions, asking for, 211–213
Pryor, Fred, 133
public information, 178
punishment, 136–137
Pygmalion (George Bernard Shaw), 122

questions, closed- vs. open-ended, 59

racism, 216–217
reinforcement, positive, 81–82
relaters, 14–16
relationship(s), 72–76
    and authority, 72–73
    "bad," 28–29
    with boss, 122
    building, 74
    with customer, 131–132
    focusing on positive elements of, 59–60
    listening for, 100
    and meetings, 69
    mentoring, 94–96
    and networking, 96–97, 224
    with other departments, 205
    personal, 74
    as power, 125
    professional, 73
reports, 30–31
reputation, 20
resources, competition for, 209
responsibility, accepting, 65–66
revenge, 197
rumors, 179

self-assessment, *see* assessment(s)
self-development, xiii

self-directed bosses, 25
self-promotion, fear of, 160
sexism, 216–217
Shaw, George Bernard, 122
Silver, Susan, on getting organized, 112
skills
    delegation, 189
    growing your, 163
    influence, 196–198
    and training, 150
slogans, 35
SMART criteria, 154, 155
social class tests, 167–168
socializing, 74
"soft" negotiation, 44–45
staff, delegating to, 193–194
staff departments, 36n.
Standard & Poor, 178
standards, performance, 2–3
standing up, 66
status symbols, 172–174
stereotypes, *see* discrimination
stress, and humor, 141
styles
    of boss, 13–17, 23–27, 223
    conflicts between, 4
    decision-making, 24
    information, 24–25
    language, 25–26
    priority, 23–24
style tests, 167–168
success
    and appearance, 217
    helping with boss's, 39–40
    mutual, xiii
supervision, 143–144
supervisor, *see* boss(es)
supportive, being, 7–9
symbolic language, 172–174

tactics, underhanded, 124–125
task-oriented project portfolios, 146

team(s)
  and humor, 141
  loyalty to, 105–106
  playing on, 8
temporary delegation, 193
ten-coin technique, 82–83
tests, hidden, 165–171
  types of, 166–168
  uncovering, 168–170
thinking outside of the box, 22
third parties, neutral, 46
threats, xi–xii, 62–64
  and conflicts, 62
  self-assessment on, 63–64
  unintentional, 63
time, spending extra, 162–163
time management, 138–139
total loyalty, 105–106, 225
total quality management (TQM), 5,
    152–153
trade groups, 10–11
trade-offs, 23
trade shows, 10
training, 150–151
Triple Constraints, 23

underhanded tactics, 124–125
understanding
  and communication skills, 135
  of departmental functions,
    204–205
  as power, 126

unethical behaviors, 21
unintentional threats, 63
Ury, William, on negotiation, 44
U.S. Code of Federal Regulations,
    173

verbal communications, paper vs.,
    30
Victory Log, 110
visiting the boss, 55–56
voice, 88

walk-away power, 45
wardrobe, 77–79
WIFM, 135
Wilson, Robert Anton, 136
win/win negotiation, 8, 44, 53, 59
women, 215
work
  doing extra, 162–164
  turning down, 134–135
work habits, good, 139
work journals, 219
work masks, 72
writing
  goal of business, 31
  as skill, 148–149

xenophobia, 218

Ziglar, Zig, 33, 163